THE BEDFORD SERIES IN HISTORY AND CULTURE

César Chávez

A Brief Biography with Documents

Related Titles in
THE BEDFORD SERIES IN HISTORY AND CULTURE
Advisory Editors: Natalie Zemon Davis, *Princeton University*
Ernest R. May, *Harvard University*
Lynn Hunt, *University of California at Los Angeles*
David W. Blight, *Amherst College*

THE BEDFORD SERIES IN HISTORY AND CULTURE

César Chávez

A Brief Biography with Documents

Edited with an Introduction by

Richard W. Etulain

University of New Mexico

BEDFORD/ST. MARTIN'S   Boston ♦ New York

For three historians of the Chicano/a experience;

Richard Griswold del Castillo
David Maciel
Vicki Ruiz

For Bedford/St. Martin's

Publisher for History: Patricia A. Rossi
Director of Development for History: Jane Knetzger
Developmental Editor: Molly E. Kalkstein
Editorial Assistant, Publishing Services: Maria Teresa Burwell
Senior Production Supervisor: Dennis J. Conroy
Project Management: Books By Design, Inc.
Text Design: Claire Seng-Niemoeller
Indexer: Books By Design, Inc.
Cover Design: Richard Emery Design, Inc.
Cover Photo: César Chávez. Bettmann/Corbis.
Composition: Stratford Publishing Services, Inc.
Printing and Binding: Haddon Craftsmen, an RR Donnelley & Sons Company

President: Charles H. Christensen
Editorial Director: Joan E. Feinberg
Director of Marketing: Karen R. Melton
Director of Editing, Design, and Production: Marcia Cohen
Manager, Publishing Services: Emily Berleth

Library of Congress Control Number: 2001093635

Copyright © 2002 by Bedford/St. Martin's

Manufactured in the United States of America.

7 6 5 4 3 2
f e d c b a

For information, write: Bedford/St. Martin's, 75 Arlington Street, Boston, MA 02116 (617-399-4000)

ISBN: 0-312-25739-2 (paperback)
      0-312-29427-1 (hardcover)

Acknowledgments

Acknowledgments and copyrights appear at the back of the book on page 129, which constitutes an extension of the copyright page.

Foreword

The Bedford Series in History and Culture is designed so that readers can study the past as historians do.

The historian's first task is finding the evidence. Documents, letters, memoirs, interviews, pictures, movies, novels, or poems can provide facts and clues. Then the historian questions and compares the sources. There is more to do than in a courtroom, for hearsay evidence is welcome, and the historian is usually looking for answers beyond act and motive. Different views of an event may be as important as a single verdict. How a story is told may yield as much information as what it says.

Along the way the historian seeks help from other historians and perhaps from specialists in other disciplines. Finally, it is time to write, to decide on an interpretation and how to arrange the evidence for readers.

Each book in this series contains an important historical document or group of documents, each document a witness from the past and open to interpretation in different ways. The documents are combined with some element of historical narrative—an introduction or a biographical essay, for example—that provides students with an analysis of the primary source material and important background information about the world in which it was produced.

Each book in the series focuses on a specific topic within a specific historical period. Each provides a basis for lively thought and discussion about several aspects of the topic and the historian's role. Each is short enough (and inexpensive enough) to be a reasonable one-week assignment in a college course. Whether as classroom or personal reading, each book in the series provides firsthand experience of the challenge—and fun—of discovering, recreating, and interpreting the past.

Natalie Zemon Davis
Ernest R. May
Lynn Hunt
David W. Blight

Preface

César Chávez (1927–1993) belongs among the most important Americans of the second half of the twentieth century. A leading reformer, a major activist, and a well-known minority leader, Chávez became the country's best-known Chicano before his death. This capsule biographical volume with documents illuminates the major contours of Chávez's notable life.

This book opens with a brief overview biography of Chávez. The first pages of this profile focus on the early years of his hardscrabble existence and carry the story into the 1950s. The middle section of the profile treats Chávez's emergence as an important leader of field workers in the 1960s and 1970s. The closing pages discuss Chávez's direction of his farmworkers' organizations and his growing importance as a Chicano citizen of national and international fame.

Part two of the book, "A Life and Its Times," presents firsthand sources that reflect a variety of viewpoints on Chávez and his times. The first two selections are by Chávez, followed by brief samples from his wife, Helen; his mentors in labor organization; his colleague Dolores Huerta; and his opponents. Taken together, these excerpts illustrate the complexities of the past, as well as divergent viewpoints about Chávez.

Part three, "An Illustrated Life," is a photo essay of the varied representations of Chávez. Organized chronologically, this part includes photographs of Chávez and images of the farmworkers' organizations and their activities. Full captions provide narrative details and analytical commentaries. Also included are questions for students to ponder as they view this portfolio.

Part four, "A Life and Its Interpreters," will aid students in understanding the concept of historiography. These selections show that historical interpretations often differ, depending on the author and the times, and demonstrate shifting as well as opposing points of view.

Part five, "Seeing a Life Whole," begins with a chronology of Chávez's life, then, through a series of questions, asks readers to think about his life and his contributions. These questions draw on the entire book, allowing instructors to bring closure to this subject before moving on to the next assignment.

Part six, "Sources for a Life," is a bibliographical essay that summarizes and evaluates the most significant books and essays about Chávez. This discussion will be particularly helpful for instructors and readers interested in pursuing further the subjects covered in this book. With careful and selective use, this bibliography can serve as a research or reference guide for brief research projects based on the primary and secondary sources gathered here.

A note on accents. I have followed the original sources in their varied uses of accent. This decision explains, for example, the inconsistency of accents in César Chávez's name.

ACKNOWLEDGMENTS

I wish to thank several readers for their useful comments on earlier versions of this project. Vicki L. Ruiz, Shirley A. Leckie, John Summers, David Key, and Cindy Tyson read and commented on parts of the book. Timothy Moy also helped with an important photograph. Staff members at Bedford/St. Martin's also furnished good advice and encouragement: Chuck Christensen, publisher; Joan Feinberg, editorial director; Katherine Kurzman and Patricia Rossi, sponsoring editors; Billy Boardman and Donna Dennison, cover designers; Emily Berleth, production manager; and Nancy Benjamin, project editor. From start to finish, Molly Kalkstein has been the best of freelance editors. Margaret Rose prepared a new essay for this volume, and Thomas Featherstone was invaluable in gathering the needed photographs. To all these colleagues, I am indeed grateful.

Richard W. Etulain

Contents

César Chávez

A Brief Biography with Documents

PART ONE

César Chávez:
Chicano Citizen

The United Farm Workers came of age in the summer of 1970. After five arduous years of negotiations, pressure, and deprivation, these farm laborers won binding contracts from several large California growers. The victorious workers were euphoric. Perhaps the UFW had arrived as an important new force on the California labor scene.

Throughout these traumatic years, César Estrada Chávez remained a central figure in a long-standing conflict between workers and growers. A quiet, self-effacing man in his early forties, Chávez had emerged in the 1950s and 1960s as a superb labor organizer and leader. Now living in the southern San Joaquin Valley in the town of Delano, Chávez must have realized how far he had come in a short time. By the early 1970s, he was the most talked-about Mexican American in the United States. Considering his modest background, Chávez's rise to fame was particularly noteworthy. During the memorable summer of 1970 and for the rest of his life, he was the emblematic Chicano citizen in the eyes of many Americans.[1]

---

[1] Throughout this book, especially in this essay, I have made extensive use of three important books on César Chávez: Jacques E. Levy, *Cesar Chavez: Autobiography of La Causa* (New York: W. W. Norton, 1975); Richard Griswold del Castillo and Richard A. Garcia, *César Chávez: A Triumph of Spirit* (Norman: University of Oklahoma Press, 1995); and Susan Ferriss and Ricardo Sandoval, *The Fight in the Fields: Cesar Chavez and the Farmworkers Movement* (New York: Harcourt Brace, 1997).

The Early Years

Chávez's earliest years reversed the American dream. Rather than climbing the ladder of economic and social success, Chávez's family descended it during the first decade of his life. These difficult experiences taught Chávez hard lessons for his adult years, but they also left stinging memories. Even in his later career, Chávez clearly remembered the events that had disrupted the lives of his parents, his siblings, and his own family after he married. Yet those early tests of his courage, morality, and persistence prepared him for his role as an advocate of the poor and the powerless.

César Chávez was born on March 31, 1927, in Yuma, Arizona. During his boyhood, his parents, Librado and Juana Chávez, operated a small grocery store and farmed a few acres nearby. When the Great Depression struck in 1929, the Chávez family, unable to pay their taxes or to secure a loan, lost their store and land. Like so many other Mexican American families without money or economic connections, they were forced into migrant labor. Leaving Arizona, they moved to California, where they weeded vegetable fields and picked fruit.

The experiences of agricultural laborers in California differed markedly from those of workers in most of the other western states. In the 1800s, large landowners in California had gobbled up enormous expanses of arable land. By contrast, in most of the Midwest and in other rich agricultural areas of the trans-Mississippi West, large tracts were divided into smaller units before being sold. Well before 1900, these land barons were hard-pressed to find the thousands of field workers they needed to clear and till their land and to harvest their abundant crops. Later, in the 1900s, as water became available for large irrigation projects in the state's interior valleys, the need for farm laborers became even greater. Beginning in the late 1930s, Chávez and his family were caught up in this prolonged search for agricultural workers in California.[2]

The first large group of field workers to answer the call were the Chinese, who appeared after the completion of the transcontinental railroad in 1869. Nearly 10,000 Chinese, who had formerly worked on the railroad, migrated to California's agricultural areas. Even though the Chinese proved to be exemplary field laborers, anti-Chinese

[2]Joan London and Henry Anderson, *So Shall Ye Reap: The Story of Cesar Chavez and the Farm Workers' Movement* (New York: Thomas Y. Crowell, 1970), 7–11; Cletus E. Daniel, *Bitter Harvest: A History of California Farm Workers, 1870–1941* (Ithaca, N.Y.: Cornell University Press, 1981).

groups, especially labor unions, lobbied to end Chinese immigration in the 1880s. Soon thereafter, Japanese workers replaced the Chinese as California's main source of field laborers. Unfortunately, racism again interfered, and this new supply of workers was soon cut off as well. By the 1920s, Chinese and Japanese immigrants were not welcome in California.

Newcomers from Mexico then replaced Asians as California's primary source of agricultural labor. Although the census recorded only 8,000 Mexicans in California in 1900, thousands more flooded north in the next generation, especially to escape the revolution that violently divided Mexico from 1910 to 1920. By 1920, nearly 100,000 Mexicans resided in California. Most of the immigrants proved to be superb field workers. Many California farmers concluded that Mexican laborers were "tractable": willing to work long hours, do difficult "stoop" labor, and forgo organizing labor unions.

In the next three decades, dramatic changes marked the experiences of Mexican farmworkers in California. Even though thousands of Mexicans and Mexican Americans were repatriated (sent back to Mexico) during the 1930s, farmworkers gained in number and strength during those years. As early as 1928, a Mexican union, 2,700 members strong, went on strike in the Imperial Valley. During the next decade, other strikes broke out in support of berry, cotton, cantaloupe, and other field workers. In the late 1930s and early 1940s, the Chávez family joined some of the unions and took part in some of the strikes.[3]

Chávez was ten when his family moved to California as farmworkers. Later he would recall, "We thought that always you had to suffer and be hungry. . . . That was our life." Following the crops, living in labor camps, forced into segregated and inferior schools, and refused seats in "Anglo only" sections of restaurants and movie houses, Chávez learned that the American dream was beyond the grasp of many poor Mexican Americans. Before he joined the U.S. Navy in 1944, he had worked for several years in California's fields, had participated in strikes, and understood the discrimination and exploitation that Mexican American workers experienced. Those injustices were burned into his consciousness.[4]

[3] J. Craig Jenkins, *The Politics of Insurgency: The Farm Worker Movement in the 1960s* (New York: Columbia University Press, 1985), 29–65.

[4] Dick Meister and Anne Loftis, *A Long Time Coming: The Struggle to Unionize America's Farm Workers* (New York: Macmillan, 1977), 110–13, quote on p. 112; London and Anderson, *So Shall Ye Reap,* 83–84.

In his late teens and early twenties, Chávez took on new responsibilities. After his brief stint in the Navy from 1944 to 1946, he returned to Delano (De *lane* o) and worked in the fields with his family. There he became reacquainted with Helen Fabela, a member of another farmworker family. After a short courtship, César and Helen Chávez were married in October 1948. At first the couple continued working in the fields. Then Chávez worked for a lumber company in northern California. After deciding that northern California was too wet and cold, they moved to San Jose, in the Bay Area. Meanwhile, their family quickly expanded. Between 1949 and 1952, four children were born to the couple. Four others arrived in the next few years.

Becoming an Organizer

In the 1950s, Chávez's life took a new turn. While he was still laboring as a field worker during the growing season and at a lumberyard during the off-season, he and his family moved to a section of San Jose known as Sal Si Puedes ("Get out if you can"). There, as devout Catholics who regularly attended Mass, César, Helen, and their growing family became well acquainted with Father Donald McDonnell. The priest was already living in the Sal Si Puedes community and urging his parishioners to work for better wages and living conditions for Mexican Americans both in his barrio (neighborhood) and in nearby bracero (field worker) camps.

Father McDonnell was also building a mission dedicated to Our Lady of Guadalupe,[5] who later became an enormously important religious, social, and political figure among Chávez's followers. By the mid-twentieth century, she was, as one writer has noted, "a strong symbolic spiritual mother ... always there to lend a helping hand to the poor." For some Mexican Americans, she was an emblem of faith and hope; for others, a symbol of their Mexican and Catholic identities; and for still others, a maternal encouragement of liberation from oppressors.[6]

---

[5]In 1531, the Virgin Mary was believed to have appeared to Juan Diego, an Aztec Indian, near Mexico City. She is said to have conveyed a message of love and compassion and a promise of help and protection to all humankind. Since then, the Virgin of Guadalupe has been revered by Mexicans and other Catholics and is the patron saint of the Americas.

[6]Andrés G. Guerrero, *A Chicano Theology* (Maryknoll, N.Y.: Orbis Books, 1987), 104.

CÉSAR CHÁVEZ: CHICANO CITIZEN

When Dolores Huerta, Chávez's coleader in the farmworkers movement, was asked about Our Lady of Guadalupe's meaning for Chávez, she said that the Virgin was "a symbol of the impossible." To the union, the Virgin symbolized "that with faith you can win. . . . In our strikes we always have the Virgin with us. That's important *palanca* [moral support]." During his marches and strikes, as well as in his office, Chávez kept symbols of the Virgin alongside other religious statues, emblems, and pictures. She was for him, and for other farmworkers, a symbol of hope and unity.[7]

One evening, Father McDonnell communicated the following message to Chávez, which Chávez vividly recalled fifteen years later.

[Father McDonnell] sat with me past midnight telling me about social justice and the Church's stand on farm labor and reading from the encyclicals of Pope Leo XIII in which he upheld labor unions. . . . I began going to the bracero camps with him to help with Mass, to the city jail with him to talk with prisoners, anything to be with him so that he could tell me more about the farm labor movement.[8]

This experience was an epiphany for Chávez. Now he understood how his religious faith might help address some of the social and economic problems Mexican Americans faced. Soon another, more secular incident transformed his life.

In 1950, a labor organizer in the San Jose area persistently sought a meeting with Chávez, thinking that Chávez could help him gain entry into the Mexican American community. At first Chávez dismissed the man as "just another social worker doing a study of farm conditions, and . . . I kept refusing to meet with him." Finally, he agreed to a meeting, but he invited some of the "rough element in San Jose" to come along and "teach the *gringo* a little bit of how we felt." But the organizer turned the tables on Chávez. "This fellow was making a lot of sense," Chávez later wrote, "and I wanted to hear what he had to say."[9]

The man, named Fred Ross, was a representative of the Community Service Organization (CSO). In the next few years, Ross served as Chávez's chief mentor in community organizing. A product of the

[7]Quoted in ibid., 105–6.
[8]Quoted in Eugene Nelson, *Huelga: The First Hundred Days of the Great Delano Grape Strike* (Delano, Calif.: Farm Worker Press, 1966), 49.
[9]César Chávez, "The Organizer's Tale," *Ramparts Magazine* (July 1966): 43–50; reprinted in *Chicano: The Evolution of a People,* Renato Rosaldo, Robert A. Calvert, and Gustav L. Seligmann, eds. (Minneapolis: Winston Press, 1973), 297–302, quote on p. 297.

prominent community organizer Saul Alinsky's Industrial Areas Foundation (IAF) in Chicago, which helped poor neighborhoods to organize so as to gain political power, Ross had moved to southern California in the early 1940s to organize Mexican Americans in the Los Angeles area. Under Ross's leadership, the CSO set out to help Mexican Americans in several ways. CSO representatives would help register new voters, defend Mexican American civil rights, end discriminatory housing practices, and investigate allegations of police brutality. Ross and the other CSO leaders were especially successful in registering Mexican Americans to vote.[10]

By the early 1950s, Ross had transferred to San Jose, where he met Chávez. In San Jose, Ross and the CSO were working with urban Mexican Americans, helping them register to vote and become more involved in social and economic issues. Immediately impressed with Ross's patience and persuasive skills, Chávez began working with him as an organizer in San Jose. It was a scary business because Chávez was by nature quiet and even shy. He did not relish the tasks of organizing meetings and buttonholing fellow Mexican Americans to attend those meetings. Yet he was convinced that Mexican Americans must become more active in community affairs.

Chávez realized, too, that his education was inadequate for his new role as an organizer. Having attended school in more than sixty classrooms while his parents moved from field to field, he had left school altogether in the seventh grade. Now he had to improve his reading and writing skills. He also learned how important public libraries could be in getting an education. Chávez studied the lives of St. Francis of Assisi, Henry David Thoreau, and Mahatma Gandhi. Their writings, as well as those of St. Paul and other Christian writers, influenced him greatly. He was particularly drawn to their ideas about social justice and nonviolence because these two subjects seemed so relevant to the experiences of Mexican Americans in California.[11]

Despite his hesitation about undertaking the demanding work, Chávez became a strong organizer. He was convinced that Mexican Americans had to organize if they were to gain more power in the United States. Chávez was so successful in registering Mexican Americans to vote that the CSO next charged him with helping Mexican immigrants gain their citizenship. Similar assignments in the suburbs of San Jose, in Oakland, and in the San Joaquin Valley soon followed.

---

[10]Griswold del Castillo and Garcia, *César Chávez,* 23–25.
[11]Ibid., 23–24; Meister and Loftis, *A Long Time Coming,* 112–13.

Using the community-organizing techniques refined by Alinsky, Chávez worked tirelessly to help Mexican Americans become active in political organizations, where he thought they could bring about needed changes in local and national politics. Even though conservatives and entrenched politicians attempted to head off the efforts of Chávez and other organizers, sometimes labeling them Communists or leftist sympathizers, the CSO succeeded in mobilizing Mexican Americans throughout California in the early 1950s.[12]

In the next few years, Chávez became a paid staff member of the CSO, moving in and out of California valley towns like a traveling salesman peddling his wares. He dragged his growing family and friends into his work. In 1958, the CSO made him a director of the nationwide group.[13] Chávez had become a model organizer and began to inspire others to join him.

Among the newcomers in his traveling band was Dolores Huerta. A young, vivacious Mexican woman, Huerta was already the mother of four children in 1957 when she met Chávez. The fiery, dependable, indefatigable Huerta was immediately impressed by his demeanor, later saying that he was "so quiet and easygoing, never got into a fight; he just did the work." The feeling was mutual. Although later they would spar on many issues and sometimes verbally attack each other, they would never lose that mutual respect. Eventually, Huerta became Chávez's most active and trusted lieutenant. She represented strong Mexican American women among farmworker and labor leadership, and she demonstrated how much Chávez came to rely on women in his work.[14]

Despite his successes, Chávez remained dissatisfied. For several years, he urged the CSO to turn its energies toward organizing a union solely for farmworkers. Among the laboring groups of California, these were the people Chávez cared about most. Although he tried exhaustively to cajole the CSO into championing farm laborers, they refused to organize the group he wanted because they wanted to focus on urban Mexican Americans. At one point, Chávez even offered to work for free for one year if the CSO would do as he asked. When

[12]John Gregory Dunne, *Delano: The Story of the California Grape Strike* (New York: Farrar, Straus and Giroux, 1967), 66–68, 69–71.
[13]Peter Matthiessen, *Sal Si Puedes: Cesar Chavez and the New American Revolution* (New York: Dell, 1969), 48–55.
[14]Margaret Rose, "Traditional and Nontraditional Patterns of Female Activism in the United Farm Workers of America, 1962 to 1980," *Frontiers* 11 (No. 1, 1990): 26–32; quote from Matthiessen, *Sal Si Puedes,* 51.

the CSO rejected his overtures once again in 1962, Chávez rose to his feet at a CSO meeting and quietly said, "I resign." It was a momentous decision. He had been affiliated with the CSO for nearly a decade; the organization had changed his life.[15]

Without much reflection and with even less financial support, Chávez struck out in a new direction. As he did so often throughout his career, he followed his head more than his billfold. Relocating to Delano, where he and his large family could count on their relatives for a place to stay and something to eat, Chávez worked to achieve his dream of a national organization for farmworkers.

Although he began his mission with enthusiasm, his prospects were quite bleak, like a woodpecker working a marble quarry. Chávez had no job and had to live on savings of only a few hundred dollars. He faced two especially vexing problems: He had no money to launch his organization, and farm laborers in Delano lacked any semblance of a group to speak for them.[16]

Despite these large problems, Chávez organized the National Farm Workers Association (NFWA) in 1962 (also known as the Farm Workers Association [FWA]). In the next two years, Chávez's possibilities of success seemed especially slim because so few workers were rallying to his cause. But his wife and older children helped support his activities by working in nearby fields. Meanwhile, Chávez labored tirelessly, meeting with workers and their families, compiling lists of prospective members for the organization, and encouraging farm families experiencing financial and health problems. Gradually, his patient manner and low-key methods helped him win hundreds of supporters. By 1964, his new FWA had enrolled more than a thousand members and had organized a credit union with $25,000 in assets. And more help was on the way.

By the 1960s, the Delano area was one of the richest grape-growing regions in central California. As many as five thousand farm laborers resided in the area, providing the needed seasonal workers in the grape industry. Most field hands worked for large agricultural businesses, such as Schenley and Di Giorgio. These large firms dominated the farm scene, controlling and treating farm laborers like serfs in a medieval fiefdom. Gradually, horror stories spread of the intransigent business control and low wages, inadequate housing, and harassment that farmworkers experienced. Soon after Chávez arrived, other

[15]Matthiessen, *Sal Si Puedes,* 52.
[16]Jenkins, *The Politics of Insurgency,* 131–32.

activists, wishing to reform these injustices, began to trickle into the area.

Several of the most important reform agencies that came to Delano were linked to churches, in part because these organizations exhibited their sympathies for field workers and their willingness to help Chávez. In 1964–65, the most notable of these groups was the Migrant Ministry, an arm of the National Council of Churches. Chávez sought the aid and support of such agencies for his group. Chris Hartmire and later the dynamic Jim Drake, both ministers affiliated with the Protestant Migrant Ministry, became notable assistants to Chávez. As historians Dick Meister and Anne Loftis observed, "By 1964, the activities of the Migrant Ministry and the NFWA were virtually inseparable."[17]

Gathering support person by person, Chávez began to think that a large strike might gain new rights for his farmworkers. His leadership of the NFWA and its growing strength illustrate the inclusiveness of his policies. At his side were several groups: his own family and other relatives; his trusted lieutenants Dolores Huerta, Gil Padilla (also a farmworker), and his cousin Manuel Chávez; a few activist priests; growing numbers of Mexican, Filipino, and other minority workers; and a notably large group of liberal Protestant ministers. At the center of this pulsating organization was Chávez. He had been offered several other positions, some paying more than $20,000 annually, but he was already tied in all ways to the NFWA. At this time, Chávez's only source of income was his $50-a-week salary from the NFWA. That was not enough to support his wife and children, so he worked in the fields alongside them as well.

By the late summer of 1965, Delano was seething with discontent and rumors of strikes. Sensational national and local happenings helped bring the situation to a boil. In these memorable months, Dr. Martin Luther King Jr. was leading civil rights marches in Alabama; boycotts, sit-ins, and other protests were erupting across the South; and Congress was passing new civil rights bills, which were signed into law by President Lyndon Johnson. In addition, the controversial war in Vietnam was heating up.

Meanwhile, the Agricultural Workers Organizing Committee (AWOC) launched a strike. Affiliated with the AFL-CIO, the AWOC, under the able and tough leadership of Filipino Larry Itliong, took on grape growers in the Delano area. AWOC members struck for better

[17]Meister and Loftis, *A Long Time Coming,* 123.

wages, and Itliong asked Chávez for his support. Chávez had to make a quick decision. He had wanted to wait until his organization was larger and much stronger, but the AWOC strike and mounting pressure demanded that Chávez decide now.

Chávez's dilemma vexed him, and he told one interviewer, "Oh, God, we're not ready for a strike." The NFWA clearly lacked the power and financial backing to undertake a long, costly strike. But if Chávez failed to support the AWOC, if he didn't take his own union out on strike, would there ever be a more auspicious moment to move? "Backed into a corner, his hand forced," he acted. On September 16, he called a meeting, and perhaps as many as fifteen hundred people filled and spilled out of Our Lady of Guadalupe Church in Delano. Chávez told those gathered, "You are here to discuss a matter which is of extreme importance to yourselves, your families, and your community." The vote to strike was unanimous.[18]

The next morning, the strike against the region's grape growers became a reality. If Chávez began the strike as a locally recognized labor organizer, he emerged five years later, when the strike finally ended, not only as the country's best-known farm labor leader but also as the most-recognized Mexican American in the United States.

When the Delano strike began in the fall of 1965, no one expected it to last five years. With less than $100 in his strike fund, Chávez was forced, despite his reluctance, to accept outside financial support. In this time of large needs, the Migrant Ministry was a bulwark for his nascent union. As Chávez wrote in 1966, the ministry forces "were the first to come to our rescue, financially and in every other way, and they spread the word to other benefactors."[19] In December 1965, Walter Reuther, head of the United Automobile Workers (UAW), came to California and promised the strikers $5,000 a month. Soon thereafter, the leadership of the AFL-CIO transferred its support from the AWOC to the NFWA. The two groups merged in summer 1966, becoming the United Farm Workers Organizing Committee (UFWOC), with the new entity receiving doubled support from the AFL-CIO. These happenings meant that within a year of the strike's beginning the Migrant Ministry and several unions, as well as other reformers and political action groups, had swung their much-needed support behind Chávez and the farmworkers. Chávez had reason to believe that the tide might be turning for his laborers.[20]

[18]Dunne, *Delano,* 79.
[19]Chávez, "The Organizer's Tale," 302.
[20]Jenkins, *The Politics of Insurgency,* 141–42.

The grape growers were not sitting on their hands, however. Buoyed by public support from businesses, religious groups, and community affiliates in the Delano area, the growers pictured the strikers as devil figures—or worse, as leftists or even Communists. They also harassed Chávez's pickets standing at the edges of fields and attempted to quiet strikers who were urging other workers to join *la huelga* (the strike). Occasionally, violence broke out on either side: Pickets tossed dirt clods and rocks at the growers, and owners or their foremen sometimes shoved or sprayed picketers and strikers with water hoses. Most of all, growers attempted to undercut the strike by hiring strikebreakers, called scabs, from other regions of California or by importing workers from Mexico. These hated newcomers agreed to replace the striking field workers. Scabs from south of the border became a career-long, unsolved problem for Chávez.[21]

As the strike dragged on, Chávez realized the need for stronger weapons to force the growers into contracts that would benefit the farmworkers. Convinced from his readings and from Catholic teachings that all his methods must be nonviolent, he turned to the boycott. It was a tactic that other unions seldom used, but one that especially appealed to Chávez. Combined, the strike and the boycott focused on the grapes and wines of Schenley Industries and the processed products of the Di Giorgio Corporation, S & W Fine Foods, and Tree-Sweet. As grocery chains, restaurants, and union groups throughout the country learned of the strike and began to boycott these products, Delano area firms saw their sales drop noticeably.[22]

To dramatize his issues, Chávez decided in early 1966 to lead a march on the state capitol in Sacramento. The *perigrinación* (march) set off in mid-March, timed to arrive at the capitol on Easter. As expected, the twenty-five-day pilgrimage was as ceremonial as it was political.[23] Important symbols of what came to be called *La Causa* (the Cause)—the Virgin of Guadalupe, presentations by El Teatro Campesino (a type of guerrilla theater), and a Lenten atmosphere—accompanied the marchers, although many supporters wanted to focus more on the strike, the boycott, and social justice than on such religious symbols.

Another important symbol for the farmworkers was the union flag, which had made its dramatic debut in September 1962. Chávez had

[21]Meister and Loftis, *A Long Time Coming,* 131–41.
[22]Ronald B. Taylor, *Chavez and the Farm Workers* (Boston: Beacon Press, 1975), 149–51.
[23]Matthiessen, *Sal Si Puedes,* 127–30.

asked his cousin Manuel Chávez to prepare a banner or flag to be displayed at the organizational meeting of the earlier FWA. He wanted a union emblem that would embody the dreams and goals of the farmworkers. Manuel Chávez's design included a black eagle on a red and white background. When the flag was unfurled in front of the convention, some people thought the design was too daring, possibly repelling rather than inviting new members. Manuel Chávez explained that the black eagle represented the "plight of the workers," white stood for hope, and red stood for "the sacrifice that would be required of them."[24]

Once the assembly understood the flag's meanings, they immediately adopted it as the union symbol. "When that damn eagle flies," Manuel told them, "we'll have a union." In their enthusiasm, the delegates also coined a *grito* (cry), which became the motto of the Union: *Viva La Causa* (Long live the cause).[25] Like the symbol of the Virgin of Guadalupe, the union flag became an emblem of unity, hope, and strength for Chávez and his farmworkers.

In Sacramento, a crowd estimated at ten thousand gathered on the capitol steps to see and greet the marchers. Although Governor Edmund G. ("Pat") Brown had conveniently fled Sacramento rather than face Chávez and his cohorts, the farmworkers won a major propaganda victory in announcing from the capitol that Schenley had capitulated and would negotiate a contract with them.[26]

Success lasted but a few days. Cries of *Viva la Huelga* and *Viva la Causa* quickly disappeared. Even though the strike and boycott had exerted noticeable pressure on the giant grower Di Giorgio, the corporation turned to the Teamsters union to negotiate a contract rather than to Chávez and the UFWOC. Then, overnight, the Teamsters rigged a vote on a new contract, which caught Chávez and his supporters off guard. Withdrawing from and picketing the vote, the UFWOC, at Chávez's insistence, appealed to Governor Brown. The governor agreed that the earlier vote, which the Teamsters had won easily, was crooked; he called for a new one. Pushed hard by Chávez, UFWOC organizers and volunteers worked long hours to win the vote. Their efforts paid off. At the end of August 1966, the UFWOC beat out the Teamsters 530 to 331 for the Di Giorgio contract.[27] Soon after the vote, Martin Luther King Jr. telegrammed congratulations to

[24] Ferriss and Sandoval, *The Fight in the Fields,* 73.
[25] Ibid., 73–74.
[26] Taylor, *Chavez and the Farm Workers,* 178–80.
[27] Ibid., 190–203.

Chávez: "You and your valiant fellow workers have demonstrated your commitment to righting grievous wrongs forced upon exploited people. We are together with you in spirit and in determination that our dreams for a better tomorrow will be realized."[28]

As King's telegram suggests, Chávez had gained a national reputation for his work among agricultural laborers. Very soon, farmworkers in Texas called on him to participate in their reform efforts. Democratic party leaders in California and elsewhere also courted his support. Catholic activists lined up to join his efforts toward social justice. But it was the farmworkers themselves who became his most loyal supporters. As author Peter Matthiessen wrote, "Their endurance and faith in Chávez were astonishing."[29] The workers had always suffered, but Chávez had linked their suffering to an admirable cause. Together, they might achieve the noteworthy goal of economic equality for the farmworkers. For Chávez, this equality meant higher wages, more job stability, better living conditions, and the end of violent harassment, especially of strikers and women.

For Chávez, strikes, boycotts, and well-publicized marches were not enough. When some of Chávez's supporters began to threaten violence, he decided to make another dramatic stand for nonviolence. He stopped eating. Inspired by Gandhi's use of fasts to inspire his followers in India, Chávez concluded that a fast would help rededicate the farmworkers to nonviolent tactics.[30] Surreptitiously beginning his fast on February 15, 1968, he called a meeting four days later and openly declared it. He would remain on his fast, Chávez said, "until such time as everyone in the strike ignored" him or "made up their minds that they were not going to be committing violence."[31]

These events brought heightened national attention to Chávez's endeavors. While on the fast, he remained at Forty Acres, the farmworker headquarters just outside Delano. There, media representatives, hundreds of his followers, and other onlookers gathered to follow the event. Some supporters, disliking the religious aura of Chávez's fasting, abandoned Delano. But on March 11, the day Chávez ended his fast, Robert Kennedy, then a leading but unannounced Democratic candidate for president, chartered a plane to join Chávez at Forty Acres (see pages 60–61). Both well-known Catholics, Chávez and Kennedy broke bread together and were surrounded by Helen

[28]Griswold del Castillo and Garcia, *César Chávez,* 57.
[29]Matthiessen, *Sal Si Puedes,* 137.
[30]Ferriss and Sandoval, *The Fight in the Fields,* 141–45.
[31]Levy, *Cesar Chavez,* 273.

Chávez, Juana Chávez (his mother), and dozens of farmworkers and their supporters. Religion, family, a spiritual quest, politics, and a labor movement were united in this one evocative, emblematic moment.

Chávez's twenty-five-day fast was the prologue to the consequential months that immediately followed. In early April, King was assassinated in Memphis. In June, Kennedy was gunned down in Los Angeles..During the late summer, the violent civil war among Democrats at their convention in Chicago and the divisive presidential campaign that led to Republican Richard Nixon's victory over Democrat Hubert Humphrey added greatly to the social turmoil disrupting the entire country. These tumultuous events also drew attention away from Chávez's efforts and thereby undercut support for them. Threats on his life and physical illnesses added to his troubles.

Throughout 1969 and the first half of 1970, the boycott wore on. Sensing that it was gradually pushing growers toward contract negotiations, Chávez tried to keep his troops behind him. In addition, he attempted to avoid disagreements with his followers over his leadership or the goals of the boycott. Gradually, by the spring of 1970, the balance of power shifted toward the workers. Grower after grower signed contracts and agreed to recognize the union by printing its black eagle on their fruit and vegetable boxes.[32]

The excitement mounted in the early summer and reached its apex in mid-July. Calling a meeting on July 16, Chávez read a message that the growers had agreed "to negotiate ... with [the] United Farm Workers Organization Committee for the purpose of effecting a labor agreement between the parties."[33] Working through exhausting day and night sessions, Chávez and twenty-three growers, who produced about half the grapes in California, finally agreed to a contract. The strike came to an end on July 29. For five years, Chávez and his cohorts had taken on the Goliaths of the California grape industry, and ultimately they won.

National Labor Leader

July 1970 was a turning point in Chávez's career. In the previous two decades, he had learned the valuable lessons of an organizer, he had become the leader of a ragtag labor union, and he had snatched a

[32] Consuelo Rodriguez, *Cesar Chavez,* Hispanics of Achievement (New York: Chelsea House, 1991), 83–85; Levy, *Cesar Chavez,* 303 ff.
[33] Quoted in Levy, *Cesar Chavez,* 315.

major victory from recalcitrant growers. By the late 1960s, Chávez had become one of the best-known Mexican Americans in the United States, *Time* magazine had named him "Man of the Year," and he symbolized for many Americans the surging power of minority leaders throughout the country. In every way, the 1960s were halcyon years for Chávez and his farmworkers.

The next two decades were less favorable. They sent him new challenges that sometimes sidetracked his best efforts. For Chávez, as for others, the disappearance of the reform-driven 1960s and the emergence of the less yeasty and more conservative 1970s and 1980s were disappointing. The issues under debate and the mood of the country changed notably after Chávez won his signal victory against the grape growers in 1970. Meanwhile, the political climate of California began moving away from Chávez and toward the more conservative Republican party.

The questions facing Chávez in the 1970s were of two kinds. First, how could he keep his farmworkers united and focused on the wage, housing, and field condition issues he thought paramount? Second, how could he beat down deadly competition from the Teamsters for control of the field workers? Chávez's reactions to these stiff challenges illuminate his burgeoning role as the most influential Chicano in the United States.

In the early 1970s, Chávez tried to repeat the methods he had used earlier to attain successes. Within a week after the contract signing at Delano, he was on the road, urging fruit pickers and lettuce workers throughout farming areas in California to stand up for their rights. In December 1970, when he was arrested for disobeying an injunction against boycotting a lettuce grower, a defiant Chávez instructed his supporters to "boycott the hell out of them."[34]

Meanwhile, he continued to garner widespread attention for his stances. In fact, he became something of a celebrity among political and cultural leaders. Religious and political figures, for example, visited him in jail. Later, his followers and other reformers compared him to Martin Luther King Jr. In 1973, Chávez worked to establish a farmworker fund in King's name and to advance nonviolent social change, causing King's widow, Coretta Scott King, to speak of Chávez as exemplifying "the true spirit of love, of truth, of justice and [one] who comes to us at this time in our history to challenge us and to remind

[34]Levy, *Cesar Chavez,* 428.

us that this spirit and this spirit alone will be the force that will bring us to the community of justice with peace and brotherhood."[35]

Ironically, at the same time that Chávez received such praise, he faced renewed competition and fresh attacks on his leadership. Again, the Teamsters challenged Chávez in the lettuce fields. He hammered out a compromise with this tough union, but his opponents soon reneged on their promises by signing "sweetheart" deals that benefited growers and the Teamsters in the mid-1970s. These jurisdictional fights took their toll on Chávez. He was trying to do too much. Attempting to keep his supporters unified and focused—they became known as the United Farm Workers (UFW) in 1972—and endeavoring to fight off the Teamsters undercut Chávez's leadership.[36] As Chicano historian Rodolfo Acuña has written, Chávez "did not delegate authority and involved himself with too much detail."[37] Some of his strongest supporters began to complain about his inadequate generalship, and membership in the UFW fell from a high of fifty thousand in 1970–71 to perhaps as low as ten thousand in 1973.

To rally his faltering troops, Chávez launched a new round of attention-catching activities. When Democratic governor Jerry Brown replaced the less sympathetic Republican Ronald Reagan in 1975, Chávez took advantage of this political shift and stepped up his efforts to push for legislation favorable to his cause. Moving in that direction, the state legislature that year enacted the California Agricultural Labor Relations Act, a notable victory for Chávez, since the law allowed farmworkers to vote in union elections. Another fast around Easter, 1975, encouraged farmworkers to avoid violence. In June of the same year, Chávez undertook a one-thousand-mile, fifty-nine-day march from the Mexican border north through central California. He also traveled to Europe to further the boycott of products grown and harvested by farmers and workers unsympathetic to the UFW cause.

In some ways, Chávez's frenetic actions drew attention away from other pressing problems. As membership dipped precipitously and criticism of Chávez's actions mounted, he drove himself to provide new recognition, support, and benefits for his field workers. Meanwhile, social and political radicals who wanted Chávez and the UFW to become an important (if not the central) unit of a larger Chicano cul-

---

[35]Quoted in John C. Hammerback and Richard J. Jensen, *The Rhetorical Career of César Chávez* (College Station: Texas A & M University Press, 1998), 101–2.

[36]Taylor, *Chavez and the Farm Workers,* 251, 259, 261–69.

[37]Rodolfo Acuña, *Occupied America: A History of Chicanos,* 3rd ed. (New York: Harper & Row, 1988), 327.

tural and political movement were upset when he resisted their efforts. His actions alienated increasing numbers of Chicanos hoping and aiming for even greater, more revolutionary reforms, including political and social movements solely for Chicano purposes.[38]

Similar successes and failures characterized Chávez's actions in the 1980s. On the one hand, the UFW claimed to have rebounded to 100,000 members early in the decade. In addition, piecework wages, health benefits, and other gains had clearly spiraled upward since the 1960s. The union also was winning elections under the Agricultural Labor Relations Board (ALRB) and generally doing quite well. Some growers even admitted that Chávez and his farmworkers had accomplished needed changes in the fields.[39]

On the other hand, several difficulties continued to beset Chávez. For one, his devoted followers, the *Chavistas,* complained that newcomers exhibited less commitment to La Causa than earlier supporters. And when Chávez tried to rally his forces with new vigor or innovative techniques, he often met with stiff resistance, some of which came from supporters who thought him too pushy. Moreover, in selecting promising newcomers for important positions, he sometimes alienated longtime followers unwilling to accept these inexperienced helpers. Others found Chávez too arbitrary, dogmatic, and selfish. On one occasion, he ripped out the phone of a coworker because he thought the man used it excessively. Chávez also took a UFW-supplied car and credit card away from a young lawyer who was, he believed, piling up large debts.[40]

Such controversies plagued Chávez until his death. Yet the conflicts never sidetracked his efforts to better the economic conditions of farmworkers or quelled his enthusiasm for undertaking new reforms. During the mid- to late 1980s, he renewed his efforts to improve living conditions for field workers. While traveling throughout interior California, he found laborers living in tin or cardboard shacks and even caves. True, workers and their children had benefited from advances in pay, fringe benefits, and medical care; but, Chávez observed, "this progress only highlight[ed] the miserable poverty too many other farmworkers still suffer[ed] in our midst." There was, he added, still too much "sexual harassment of women workers; . . . high infant

---

[38]Juan Gómez-Quiñones, *Chicano Politics: Reality and Promise, 1940–1990* (Albuquerque: University of New Mexico Press, 1990), 133–34, 137–38.

[39]Ferriss and Sandoval, *The Fight in the Fields,* 221ff.

[40]Griswold del Castillo and Garcia, *César Chávez,* 132–33; Ferriss and Sandoval, *The Fight in the Fields,* 223.

mortality; short life expectancy," and too many workers and their families "living out in canyons and under trees."[41]

Chávez also turned his attention to another threat to farmworkers—the excessive and deadly use of pesticides in California fields. Although Governor George Deukmejian tried in the mid-1980s to block UFW challenges to pesticide use by growers, Chávez jumped into the controversial fray, with considerable success. Strong opposition kept Chávez from winning outright, but later journalists and policymakers agreed that his early efforts had laid the groundwork for subsequent legislation that would outlaw or limit the uses of several dangerous pesticides.[42]

Chávez next ran headlong into another vexing problem. Floods of immigrants from Mexico—some with work permits, others arriving illegally—were hamstringing Chávez's strike and boycott efforts in California and across the Southwest. He tried in vain to stem the tide of undocumented workers, especially those hired as strikebreakers. Reports came out that Chávez turned his head on occasion when his supporters used violence against illegal workers. Manuel Chávez was even accused of attacking strikebreakers attempting to cross the Rio Grande into the United States. César Chávez talked with Mexican officials about the problem and even visited Mexico in an attempt to stop the flow of illegal workers, but they posed then, as they do today, an unresolved dilemma.

By the beginning of the 1990s, Chávez had become a different man from the one who had led the famed Delano strike of the late 1960s. He was now in his mid-sixties, his health was uncertain, and some people thought that his energy was flagging. Continuing attacks by social critics and journalists also spawned new tensions between Chávez and his former lieutenants. Then, in 1991, a California district court upheld an earlier decision against the UFW. As a result of that judgment, Chávez's union was eventually assessed more than $2 million in damages for their activities and the death of a worker during a strike in 1979.

The changing conservative climate in the United States added to Chávez's difficulties. Generally in the 1980s and early 1990s, Americans were less sympathetic to unions. As one account explains, "César's message was muffled by the changing times."[43] Conservatives such as the former governor and later U.S. president Ronald Reagan and other

[41]Ferriss and Sandoval, *The Fight in the Fields,* 242.
[42]Ibid., 237–39.
[43]Ibid., 237.

California governors George Deukmejian and Pete Wilson did not favor strong unions. Instead, they were more inclined to support growers and businessmen opposed to Chávez and the UFW.

Still, Chávez remained confident and active up to his last days. He launched new strikes and boycotts, took additional actions against pesticides, and traveled widely to stump for other social justice issues. In one show of strength in 1992, for example, more than ten thousand people assembled to protest for improved field conditions in California's Salinas Valley. Chávez urged his followers not to give up, and he tried to practice what he preached.

The end came unexpectedly in the spring of 1993. In April, Chávez traveled to Arizona to help farmworkers there who were being sued by a lettuce grower. Hoping to inspire the workers and to revive his own spirits, he began a fast. His friends begged him to break the fast when they observed his failing strength. On April 23, he ended the fast, went to bed exhausted, and died in his sleep.

News of Chávez's death traveled like a tragic explosion. Circulating almost as quickly were hundreds of salutes to his life and career. President Bill Clinton spoke of Chávez as an "authentic hero," and other American and world leaders compared him to Martin Luther King Jr. and Gandhi. Even more moving were the tributes from the field workers themselves. One stated simply, "For all the workers, César was strong." Another said, "God has taken the strongest arm that we have, but we will continue."[44]

The powerful and widely known, as well as the humble and unknown, paid their respects at Chávez's funeral. A crowd of more than thirty thousand gathered at Delano and marched with the simple pine casket to the former UFW headquarters at Forty Acres. Chávez's family, fellow workers, members of the Kennedy family, close friends such as Dolores Huerta and Luís Valdez (the leader of El Teatro Campesino), and many others remembered their fallen leader. His life had ended, but his moral character and his role as the preeminent Chicano citizen of the late 1900s were his legacy.

César Chávez: The Man

When people met César Chávez for the first time, they often wondered how this small, quiet, modest man could have gained such an impressive reputation as a notable labor organizer and leader. By what

[44]Griswold del Castillo and Garcia, *César Chávez,* 173–74.

means had this unprepossessing, self-educated Mexican American become the most powerful minority labor leader of post–World War II America? Many others, during Chávez's lifetime and since, have raised the same questions.

Quite simply, these observers, thinking that physical appearance defines a person, could not see the experiences, ambition, and courage that shaped and drove Chávez. True, he was small in stature, and his arduous labor in the fields, his tendency to overwork, and his periodic fasts and marches often undermined his health. On numerous occasions, back problems and other health-related issues also marred his physical appearance.

Yet those closest to Chávez commented much more often on the desires and ambitions that powered his efforts, and on the quiet but fierce determination and the modest but courageous spirit that possessed him, rather than on his physical being. Early on, Chávez had learned a demanding work ethic from his grandparents, parents, and other field workers. He always worked long hours. Even after he left the fields to serve as an organizer and administrator, he often began work at four or five in the morning and continued until midnight or later. CSO leader Fred Ross was greatly impressed with Chávez's understanding of the value of work. Chávez believed in the importance of demanding, redemptive labor. But he also believed that laborers deserved fair pay for their work, help with their basic needs, and justice in their dealings with growers, businessmen, and the legal system.

If a work ethic motivated Chávez, so did the Catholic teachings that his grandmother and mother reinforced in their homes. He would never abandon his devotion to the Roman Catholic Church. Over the years, he was drawn to the church's teachings on social justice for the poor and to the Virgin of Guadalupe as a maternal, uniting, and encouraging spiritual symbol for all people of Hispanic or Catholic heritage. Indeed, Chávez's unwavering commitment to the social and moral teachings of the church were sometimes too much for his secular colleagues. They often chafed under what they considered his restrictive ties to his Catholic beliefs.

Equally important to the formation of Chávez's character was his reading. Although he failed to gain a sound education in the public schools, he eventually became a devoted reader. Educating himself in public libraries and elsewhere, he was particularly drawn to the writings of religious authors such as St. Paul and St. Francis of Assisi, as well as to the works of Henry David Thoreau, Mahatma Gandhi, and Martin Luther King Jr. These thinkers helped Chávez understand important links between religious and moral teachings and social and legal reforms. Undoubtedly, the prison writings of St. Paul, Thoreau, and King also spoke to Chávez when he himself was jailed.

Chávez's strong work ethic, his religiosity, and his self-education gradually jelled into a credo of moral values. On one occasion, when opponents were threatening his life and critics were attacking his beliefs, he told journalist Peter Matthiessen, "You are welcome to my life, but not to my principles." Examining Chávez's commitment to a few moral stances, Matthiessen wrote, "Cesar is so intensely *present* that talking to him is like going to a source, a mountain spring; one comes away refreshed."[45] Paramount among these moral beliefs was the need for justice. He informed one of his lieutenants, when he faced a particularly difficult injunction, that "men who are seeking justice are not going to be stopped by unjust decisions."[46]

Once convinced of the rightness of his stances, Chávez could be an unmovable force. If growers complained that Dolores Huerta had become unreasonable and unwilling to compromise, Chávez warned that they had better agree with Huerta because he would demand even more at the negotiating table. This stubbornness, argued his critics, sometimes led to obstinate actions. At his worst, they said, he was both blind to differences of opinion and pigheaded.

Chávez, of course, spoke from a different perspective. He had to be a tough negotiator, he asserted, because his opponents were powerful, self-interested men. He had to be relentless in his demands because growers and other agribusiness officials, driven by profits, were unwilling to grant field workers their fair share of those profits. He would accept his limitations as a leader but never give way to those who called for less dedication to his cause. From his perspective, he always had to keep his eyes on the "sweet grapes of justice." He insisted on sacrifice—his "commitment was total"—because unwavering dedication was necessary to right centuries-old injustices.[47] As supporters and critics alike learned, he might be a "small piece of skin" and a "few bones," but he was also "very, very tough."[48]

---

[45] Matthiessen, *Sal Si Puedes,* 357.
[46] Levy, *Cesar Chavez,* 389.
[47] Levy, *Cesar Chavez,* 403; Jenkins, *The Politics of Insurgency,* 135.
[48] Matthiessen, *Sal Si Puedes,* 356.

César Chávez: Chicano Citizen

In the days immediately following Chávez's death in 1993, journalists and historians seemed puzzled about how to assess his significance in American history. Should he be considered a hero? Was he significant beyond his importance to Mexican American field workers? What were the keys to his successes? Might one speak of Chávez's legacy, and if so, what were the major parts of that legacy? Nearly a decade later, these important questions still face those wishing to understand whether and how Chávez shaped recent American history.

From the beginning, one must understand that Chávez believed that ideas had consequences. He could, like Ralph Waldo Emerson, think that ideas were transcendent; but he was more convinced, like Thoreau and King, that notions put into action were much more significant. Applied to his own career, this axiom meant that convictions about social justice had to be applied practically to American society if they were to carry much meaning. Principles led to participation. He accepted poverty, jailing, and criticism if these punishing blows meant that his theories were becoming actions. Tough talk, demanding negotiations, and innumerable conflicts were logical—and expected—outcomes of putting ideas to work.

Chávez was also a man of inclusion. Throughout his career, he found ways to include in his groups men and women of varied religious, ethnic, class, and educational backgrounds—even if they were at odds with his own experiences. The UFW, as well as earlier farmworker organizations Chávez led, served as umbrella groups for Filipinos, African Americans, Puerto Ricans, poor whites, and others. He also encouraged people variously calling themselves Mexicans, Mexican Americans, Chicanos, Hispanics, Latinos, and Spanish to participate in his efforts.

In fact, Chávez avoided turning his labor organizations into nationalistic ethnic groups. When activist Chicanos spoke of *La Raza* (people of Mexican heritage) as a separatist, nationalist group, Chávez opposed them. "When La Raza means or implies racism, we don't support it," Chávez said. "If it means our struggle, our dignity, or our cultural roots, then we're for it."[49] Chávez indicated repeatedly that he led inclusive organizations, as long as prospective members supported the goals of farmworkers.

Women also played central roles in Chávez's career. His wife, Helen, served in a "traditional" capacity, which, according to one

[49]Levy, *Cesar Chavez,* 42.

scholar, meant juggling "the competing demands of family life, sexual division of labor, and protest in a unique blend of union activism." Preferring to keep house and nurture her children, Helen also served as bookkeeper for the UFW. Conversely, Dolores Huerta worked in a "nontraditional" capacity. As chief negotiator for the farmworkers, she was perhaps the most important leader next to Chávez in these groups. Although far fewer women than men were among the leadership of the UFW, throughout his career Chávez encouraged women's participation, whether in traditional or nontraditional roles.[50]

Equally inclusive were Chávez's connections with church groups. As a devout Roman Catholic, he called on priests and laypersons in parishes throughout California and beyond to support his farmworkers. But his ties to the Catholic Church did not alienate him from other religious organizations. Numerous ministers and parishioners from liberal and mainstream Protestant churches also participated in the UFW and Chávez's earlier organizations. Some, like Jim Drake, were major figures in these movements. Chávez also learned much from conservative Protestants such as the Pentecostals and from Jewish groups. On several occasions, he saluted all religious groups for their support of his people and programs. For Chávez, religion was "a powerful moral and spiritual force" that no movement could afford to overlook.[51]

In the end, Chávez appealed to and attracted a wide base of supporters. By attracting people from varied ethnic, racial, class, gender, and religious backgrounds, he repeatedly demonstrated his openness and acceptance of others. As a tireless worker and reformer, he sparked unusual devotion among his followers. He depended on personal contact and encouragement—what Evangelicals call "friendship evangelism"—to win new converts to his cause. As a moralist, he urged laborers to avoid violence, selfishness, and racism, even as he pushed them to stand up for their rights. As an idealist, he provided encouragement and hope. In the midst of one taxing situation, his clear courage and optimism, a journalist has written, indicated that Chávez would not "give up hope for a new America."[52]

[50]Rose, "Traditional and Nontraditional Patterns," 26; Vicki L. Ruiz, *From Out of the Shadows: Mexican Women in Twentieth-Century America* (New York: Oxford University Press, 1998), 134–35.

[51]César Chávez, "The Mexican-American and the Church," *El Grito* 1 (Summer 1968): 9–12, reprinted in *Voices: Readings from El Grito: A Journal of Contemporary Mexican American Thought 1967–1973,* ed. Octavio Ignacio Romano-V (Berkeley, Calif.: Quinto Sol Publications, 1971, 1973), 215.

[52]Matthiessen, *Sal Si Puedes,* 45.

Obviously, Chávez left a large legacy. He never forgot his humble beginnings when his later successes came. Even though he worked primarily with people whose experiences were similar to his, he saw their lives as part of the more equitable, less violent America of which he dreamed. In truth, he was a model Chicano citizen, hoping to increase the participation of his compatriots in the political, economic, and social systems of the larger host society. Chávez was a "liberal hero" and "social visionary," but he also was a man of vigilance and moral vision.[53]

[53]Hammerback and Jensen, *The Rhetorical Career of César Chávez,* 101.

PART TWO

A Life and Its Times

A full understanding of important historical characters demands that readers examine a variety of oral and written sources. Students and scholars alike need to listen to the voices of central protagonists, as well as those of their colleagues and opponents. Clearly, a chorus of supporting and antagonistic viewpoints helps to broaden and enrich the biographies of major historical figures.

To be able to comprehend César Chávez's notable role in recent American history, a deeper look that incorporates primary source documents is imperative. Even though Chávez himself provided few written commentaries on his life and ideas, his family members and friends, his colleagues, and even some of his opponents left valuable reminiscences of their work with him. Taken together, these primary sources provide the kind of varied, complex information students need to make informed judgments about Chávez's life.

Questions for Consideration

1. What are the most important lessons César Chávez learned in becoming a labor organizer?
2. Why did Chávez consider religious organizations—Catholic, Protestant, and others—important in his efforts as a reformer and farmworker activist?
3. What similarities and differences are evident in the remembrances of Helen Chávez and Dolores Huerta, the two most influential women in Chávez's career?

4. What do the recollections of the Reverend James Drake and journalist Jacques Levy tell you about Chávez's humanity?
5. What are the most important points Chávez made in his interview with Studs Terkel?
6. Consider the complaints that Jack King and Allan Grant, Chávez's opponents, lodged against him. Do you agree with these criticisms?

CÉSAR CHÁVEZ

The Organizer's Tale

July 1966

This brief essay, which originally appeared in Ramparts Magazine, *is one of the few Chávez wrote about himself. It reveals a good deal about his role as a community and labor organizer in the 1950s and 1960s. We learn much about his initial organizing efforts in the cities of San Jose and Oakland and in the fields of central California. Especially revealing are the accounts of people such as the Reverend James Drake, Dolores Huerta, and Helen Fabela Chávez, who supported his efforts. Chávez's ambition, courage, and commitment to his causes fill these pages.*

It really started for me 16 years ago in San Jose, California, when I was working on an apricot farm. We figured he was just another social worker doing a study of farm conditions, and I kept refusing to meet with him. But he was persistent. Finally, I got together some of the rough element in San Jose. We were going to have a little reception for him to teach the *gringo* a little bit of how we felt. There were about thirty of us in the house, young guys mostly. I was supposed to give them a signal—change my cigarette from my right hand to my left, and then we were going to give him a lot of hell. But he started talking and the more he talked, the more wide-eyed I became and the less inclined I was to give the signal. A couple of guys who were pretty drunk at the time still wanted to give the *gringo* the business, but we

César Chávez, "The Organizer's Tale," reprinted in Renato Rosaldo, Robert A. Calvert, and Gustav L. Seligmann, eds. *Chicano: The Evolution of a People* (Minneapolis: Winston Press, 1973), 297–302.

got rid of them. This fellow was making a lot of sense, and I wanted to hear what he had to say.

His name was Fred Ross, and he was an organizer for the Community Service Organization (CSO) which was working with Mexican Americans in the cities. I became immediately really involved. Before long I was heading a voter registration drive. All the time I was observing the things Fred did, secretly, because I wanted to learn how to organize, to see how it was done. I was impressed with his patience and understanding of people. I thought this was a tool, one of the greatest things he had.

It was pretty rough for me at first. I was changing and had to take a lot of ridicule from the kids my age, the rough characters I worked with in the fields. They would say, "Hey, big shot. Now that you're a *politico,* why are you working here for 65 cents an hour?" I might add that our neighborhood had the highest percentage of San Quentin graduates. It was a game among the *pachucos** in the sense that we defended ourselves from outsiders, although inside the neighborhood there was not a lot of fighting.

After six months of working every night in San Jose, Fred assigned me to take over the CSO chapter in Decoto. It was a tough spot to fill. I would suggest something, and people would say, "No, let's wait till Fred gets back," or "Fred wouldn't do it that way." This is pretty much a pattern with people, I discovered, whether I was put in Fred's position, or later, when someone else was put in my position. After the Decoto assignment I was sent to start a new chapter in Oakland. Before I left, Fred came to a place in San Jose called the Hole-in-the-Wall and we talked for half an hour over coffee. He was in a rush to leave, but I wanted to keep him talking; I was that scared of my assignment.

There were hard times in Oakland. First of all, it was a big city and I'd get lost every time I went anywhere. Then I arranged a series of house meetings. I would get to the meeting early and drive back and forth past the house, too nervous to go in and face the people. Finally I would force myself to go inside and sit in a corner. I was quite thin then, and young, and most of the people were middle-aged. Someone would say, "Where's the organizer?" And I would pipe up, "Here I am." Then they would say in Spanish—these were very poor people and we hardly spoke anything but Spanish—"Ha! This *kid?*" Most of them

pachucos: young Mexican Americans who dress and act flamboyantly and often belong to gangs

said they were interested, but the hardest part was to get them to start pushing themselves, on their own initiative.

The idea was to set up a meeting and then get each attending person to call his own house meeting, inviting new people—a sort of chain letter effect. After a house meeting I would lie awake going over the whole thing, playing the tape back, trying to see why people laughed at one point, or why they were for one thing and against another. I was also learning to read and write, those late evenings. I had left school in the 7th grade after attending sixty-seven different schools, and my reading wasn't the best.

At our first organizing meeting we had 368 people: I'll never forget it because it was very important to me. You eat your heart out; the meeting is called for 7 o'clock and you start to worry about 4. You wait. Will they show up? Then the first one arrives. By 7 there are only 20 people, you have everything in order, you have to look calm. But little by little they filter in and at a certain point you know it will be a success.

After four months in Oakland, I was transferred. The chapter was beginning to move on its own, so Fred assigned me to organize the San Joaquin Valley. Over the months I developed what I used to call schemes or tricks—now I call them techniques—of making initial contacts. The main thing in convincing someone is to spend time with him. It doesn't matter if he can read, write or even speak well. What is important is that he is a man and second, that he has shown some initial interest. One good way to develop leadership is to take a man with you in your car. And it works a lot better if you're doing the driving; that way you are in charge. You drive, he sits there, and you talk. These little things were very important to me; I was caught in a big game by then, figuring out what makes people work. I found that if you work hard enough you can usually shake people into working too, those who are concerned. You work harder and they work harder still, up to a point and then they pass you. Then, of course, they're on their own.

I also learned to keep away from the established groups and so-called leaders, and to guard against philosophizing. Working with low-income people is very different from working with the professionals, who like to sit around talking about how to play politics. When you're trying to recruit a farmworker, you have to paint a little picture, and then you have to color the picture in. We found out that the harder a guy is to convince, the better leader or member he becomes. When you exert yourself to convince him, you have his confidence and he has good motivation. A lot of people who say OK right away wind up hanging around the office, taking up the workers' time.

During the McCarthy era in one Valley town, I was subjected to a lot of redbaiting.* We had been recruiting people for citizenship classes at the high school when we got into a quarrel with the naturalization examiner. He was rejecting people on the grounds that they were just parroting what they learned in citizenship class. One day we had a meeting about it in Fresno, and I took along some of the leaders of our local chapter. Some redbaiting official gave us a hard time, and the people got scared and took his side. They did it because it seemed easy at the moment, even though they knew that sticking with me was the right thing to do. It was disgusting. When we left the building they walked by themselves ahead of me as if I had some kind of communicable disease. I had been working with these people for three months and I was very sad to see that. It taught me a great lesson.

That night I learned that the chapter officers were holding a meeting to review my letters and printed materials to see if I really was a Communist. So I drove out there and walked right in on their meeting. I said, "I hear you've been discussing me, and I thought it would be nice if I was here to defend myself. Not that it matters that much to you or even to me, because as far as I'm concerned you are a bunch of cowards." At that they began to apologize. "Let's forget it," they said. "You're a nice guy." But I didn't want apologies. I wanted a full discussion. I told them I didn't give a damn, but that they had to learn to distinguish fact from what appeared to be a fact because of fear. I kept them there till two in the morning. Some of the women cried. I don't know if they investigated me any further, but I stayed on another few months and things worked out.

This was not an isolated case. Often when we'd leave people to themselves they would get frightened and draw back into their shells where they had been all the years. And I learned quickly that there is no real appreciation. Whatever you do, and no matter what reasons you may give to others, you do it because you want to see it done, or maybe because you want power. And there shouldn't be any appreciation, understandably. I know good organizers who were destroyed, washed out, because they expected people to appreciate what they'd done. Anyone who comes in with the idea that farmworkers are free of sin and that the growers are all bastards, either has never dealt with the situation or is an idealist of the first order. Things don't work that way.

*redbaiting: accusing or attacking as a Communist

For more than ten years I worked for the CSO. As the organization grew, we found ourselves meeting in fancier and fancier motels and holding expensive conventions. Doctors, lawyers and politicians began joining. They would get elected to some office in the organization and then, for all practical purposes, leave. Intent on using the CSO for their own prestige purposes, these "leaders," many of them, lacked the urgency we had to have. When I became general director I began to press for a program to organize farmworkers into a union, an idea most of the leadership opposed. So I started a revolt within the CSO. I refused to sit at the head table at meetings, refused to wear a suit and tie, and finally I even refused to shave and cut my hair. It used to embarrass some of the professionals. At every meeting I got up and gave my standard speech: we shouldn't meet in fancy motels, we were getting away from the people, farmworkers had to be organized. But nothing happened. In March of '62 I resigned and came to Delano to begin organizing the Valley on my own.

By hand I drew a map of all the towns between Arvin and Stockton — 86 of them, including farming camps — and decided to hit them all to get a small nucleus of people working in each. For six months I traveled around, planting an idea. We had a simple questionnaire, a little card with space for name, address and how much the worker thought he ought to be paid. My wife, Helen, mimeographed them, and we took our kids for two or three day jaunts to these towns, distributing the cards door-to-door and to camps and groceries.

Some 80,000 cards were sent back from eight Valley counties. I got a lot of contacts that way, but I was shocked at the wages the people were asking. The growers were paying $1 and $1.15, and maybe 95 percent of the people thought they should be getting only $1.25. Sometimes people scribbled messages on the cards: "I hope to God we win" or "Do you think we can win?" or "I'd like to know more." So I separated the cards with the pencilled notes, got in my car and went to those people.

We didn't have any money at all in those days, none for gas and hardly any for food. So I went to people and started asking for food. It turned out to be about the best thing I could have done, although at first it's hard on your pride. Some of our best members came in that way. If people give you their food, they'll give you their hearts. Several months and many meetings later we had a working organization, and this time the leaders were the people.

None of the farmworkers had collective bargaining contracts, and I thought it would take ten years before we got that first contract.

I wanted desperately to get some color into the movement, to give people something they could identify with, like a flag. I was reading some books about how various leaders discovered what colors contrasted and stood out the best. The Egyptians had found that a red field with a white circle and a black emblem in the center crashed into your eyes like nothing else. I wanted to use the Aztec eagle in the center, as on the Mexican flag. So I told my cousin Manuel, "Draw an Aztec eagle." Manuel had a little trouble with it, so we modified the eagle to make it easier for people to draw.

The first big meeting of what we decided to call the National Farm Workers Association was held in September 1962, at Fresno, with 287 people. We had our huge red flag on the wall, with paper tacked over it. When the time came, Manuel pulled a cord ripping the paper off the flag and all of a sudden it hit the people. Some of them wondered if it was a Communist flag, and I said it probably looked more like a neo-Nazi emblem than anything else. But they wanted an explanation, so Manuel got up and said, "When that damn eagle flies—that's when the farmworkers' problems are going to be solved."

One of the first things I decided was that outside money wasn't going to organize people, at least not in the beginning. I even turned down a grant from a private group—$50,000 to go directly to organize farmworkers—for just this reason. Even when there are no strings attached, you are still compromised because you feel you have to produce immediate results. This is bad, because it takes a long time to build a movement, and your organization suffers if you get too far ahead of the people it belongs to. We set the dues at $42 a year per family, really a meaningful dues, but of the 212 we got to pay, only 12 remained by June of '63. We were discouraged at that, but not enough to make us quit.

Money was always a problem. Once we were facing a $180 gas bill on a credit card I'd got a long time ago and was about to lose. And we *had* to keep that credit card. One day my wife and I were picking cotton, pulling bolls, to make a little money to live on. Helen said to me, "Do you put all this in the bag, or just the cotton?" I thought she was kidding and told her to throw the whole boll in so that she had nothing but a sack of bolls at the weighing. The man said, "Whose sack is this?" I said, well, my wife's, and he told us we were fired. "Look at all that crap you brought in," he said. Helen and I started laughing. We were going anyway. We took the $4 we had earned and spent it at a grocery store where they were giving away a $100 prize. Each time you shopped they'd give you one of the letters of M-O-N-E-Y or a flag:

you had to have M-O-N-E-Y plus the flag to win. Helen had already collected the letters and just needed the flag. Anyway, they gave her the
ticket. She screamed, "A flag? I don't believe it," ran in and got the
$100. She said, "Now we're going to eat steak." But I said no, we're
going to pay the gas bill. I don't know if she cried, but I think she did.

It was rough in those early years. Helen was having babies and I
was not there when she was at the hospital. But if you haven't got
your wife behind you, you can't do many things. There's got to be
peace at home. So I did, I think, a fairly good job of organizing her.
When we were kids, she lived in Delano and I came to town as a
migrant. Once on a date we had a bad experience about segregation at
a movie theater, and I put up a fight. We were together then, and still
are. I think I'm more of a pacifist than she is. Her father, Fabela, was
a colonel with Pancho Villa in the Mexican Revolution. Sometimes
she gets angry and tells me, "These scabs—you should deal with
them sternly," and I kid her, "It must be too much of that Fabela blood
in you."

The movement really caught on in '64. By August we had a thousand members. We'd had a beautiful 90-day drive in Corcoran, where
they had the Battle of the Corcoran Farm Camp 30 years ago, and by
November we had assets of $25,000 in our credit union, which helped
to stabilize the membership. I had gone without pay the whole of
1963. The next year the members voted me a $40 a week salary, after
Helen had to quit working in the fields to manage the credit union.

Our first strike was in May of '65, a small one but it prepared us for
the big one. A farmworker from McFarland named Epifanio Camacho
came to see me. He said he was sick and tired of how people working
the roses were being treated, and he was willing to "go the limit." I
assigned Manuel and Gilbert Padilla to hold meetings at Camacho's
house. The people wanted union recognition, but the real issue, as in
most cases when you begin, was wages. They were promised $9 a
thousand, but they were actually getting $6.50 and $7 for grafting
roses. Most of them signed cards giving us the right to bargain for
them. We chose the biggest company, with about 85 employees, not
counting the irrigators and supervisors, and we held a series of meetings to prepare the strike and call the vote. There would be no picket
line; everyone pledged on their honor not to break the strike.

Early on the first morning of the strike, we sent out ten cars to
check the people's homes. We found lights in five or six homes and
knocked on the doors. The men were getting up and we'd say, "Where
are you going?" They would dodge, "Oh, uh . . . I was just getting up,

you know." We'd say, "Well, you're not going to work, are you?" And they'd say no. Dolores Huerta, who was driving the green panel truck, saw a light in one house where four rose-workers lived. They told her they were going to work, even after she reminded them of their pledge. So she moved the truck so it blocked their driveway, turned off the key, put it in her purse and sat there alone.

That morning the company foreman was madder than hell and refused to talk to us. None of the grafters had shown up for work. At 10:30 we started to go to the company office, but it occurred to us that maybe a woman would have a better chance. So Dolores knocked on the office door, saying, "I'm Dolores Huerta from the National Farm Workers Association." "Get out!" the man said, "you Communist. Get out!" I guess they were expecting us, because as Dolores stood arguing with him the cops came and told her to leave. She left.

For two days the fields were idle. On Wednesday they recruited a group of Filipinos from out of town who knew nothing of the strike, maybe 35 of them. They drove through escorted by three sheriff's patrol cars, one in front, one in the middle and one at the rear with a dog. We didn't have a picket line, but we parked across the street and just watched them go through, not saying a word. All but seven stopped working after half an hour, and the rest had quit by mid-afternoon.

The company made an offer the evening of the fourth day, a package deal that amounted to a 120 percent wage increase, but no contract. We wanted to hold out for a contract and more benefits, but a majority of the rose-workers wanted to accept the offer and go back. We are a democratic union so we had to support what they wanted to do. They had a meeting and voted to settle. Then we had a problem with a few militants who wanted to hold out. We had to convince them to go back to work, as a united front, because otherwise they would be canned. So we worked—Tony Orendain and I, Dolores and Gilbert, Jim Drake and all the organizers—knocking on doors till two in the morning, telling people, "You have to go back or you'll lose your job." And they did. They worked.

Our second strike, and our last before the big one at Delano, was in the grapes at Martin's Ranch last summer. The people were getting a raw deal there, being pushed around pretty badly. Gilbert went out to the field, climbed on top of a car and took a strike vote. They voted unanimously to go out. Right away they started bringing in strikebreakers, so we launched a tough attack on the labor contractors, distributed leaflets portraying them as really low characters. We attacked one—Luis Campos—so badly that he just gave up the job, and he took twenty-seven of his men out with him. All he asked was that we distribute another leaflet reinstating him in the community. And we did. What was unusual was that the grower would talk to us. The grower kept saying, "I can't pay. I just haven't got the money." I guess he must have found the money somewhere, because we were asking $1.40 and we got it.

We had just finished the Martin strike when the Agricultural Workers Organizing Committee (AFL-CIO) started a strike against the grape growers, Di Giorgio, Schenley liquors and small growers, asking $1.40 an hour and 25 cents a box. There was a lot of pressure from our members for us to join the strike, but we had some misgivings. We didn't feel ready for a big strike like this one, one that was sure to last a long time. Having no money—just $87 in the strike fund—meant we'd have to depend on God knows who.

Eight days after the strike started—it takes time to get 1,200 people together from all over the Valley—we held a meeting in Delano and voted to go out. I asked the membership to release us from the pledge not to accept outside money, because we'd need it now, a lot of it. The help came. It started because of the close, and I would say even beautiful relationship that we've had with the Migrant Ministry for some years. They were the first to come to our rescue, financially and in every other way, and they spread the word to other benefactors.

We had planned, before, to start a labor school in November. It never happened, but we have the best labor school we could ever have, in the strike. The strike is only a temporary condition, however. We have over 3,000 members spread out over a wide area, and we have to service them when they have problems. We get letters from New Mexico, Colorado, Texas, California, from farmworkers saying, "We're getting together and we need an organizer." It kills you when you haven't got the personnel and resources. You feel badly about not sending an organizer because you look back and remember all the difficulty you had in getting two or three people together, and here *they're* together. Of course, we're training organizers, many of them younger than I was when I started in CSO. They can work 20 hours a day, sleep four and be ready to hit it again; when you get to be 39 it's a different story.

The people who took part in the strike and the march have something more than their material interest going for them. If it were only material, they wouldn't have stayed on the strike long enough to win. It is difficult to explain. But it flows out in the ordinary things they say. For instance, some of the younger guys are saying, "Where do you think's going to be the next strike?" I say, "Well, we have to win in Delano." They say, "We'll win, but where do we go next?" I say, "Maybe most of us will be working in the fields." They say, "No, I don't want to go and work in the fields. I want to organize. There are a lot of people that need our help." So I say, "You're going to be pretty poor then, because when you strike you don't have much money." They say they don't care about that.

And others are saying, "I have friends who are working in Texas. If we could only help them." It is bigger, certainly, than just a strike. And if this spirit grows within the farm labor movement, one day we can use the force that we have to help correct a lot of things that are wrong in this society. But that is for the future. Before you can run, you have to learn to walk.

There are vivid memories from my childhood—what we had to go through because of low wages and the conditions, basically because there was no union. I suppose if I wanted to be fair I could say that I'm trying to settle a personal score. I could dramatize it by saying that I want to bring social justice to farmworkers. But the truth is that I went through a lot of hell, and a lot of people did. If we can even the score a little for the workers then we are doing something. Besides, I don't know any other work I like to do better than this. I really don't, you know.

CÉSAR CHÁVEZ

The Mexican American and the Church

1968

Throughout his career, Chávez relied on his enduring commitments to religion, labor activism, and social justice. As this brief piece indicates, he wanted Catholics, Protestants, and Jews to become involved in the vexing social and economic problems of Mexican Americans. He urged his followers not to overlook the spiritual, economic, and political power that churches and religiously committed people could share with needy

César Chávez, "The Mexican-American and the Church," reprinted in *Voices: Readings from El Grito: A Journal of Contemporary Mexican American Thought 1967–1973*, ed. Octavio Ignacio Romano-V (Berkeley, Calif.: Quinto Sol Publications, 1971, 1973), 215–18.

farmworkers. Chávez wrote this article during a twenty-five-day "spiritual fast" and presented it at the Second Annual Mexican-American Conference in Sacramento, California, in March 1968.

The place to begin is with our own experience with the Church in the strike which has gone on for thirty-one months in Delano. For in Delano the Church has been involved with the poor in a unique way which should stand as a symbol to other communities. Of course, when we refer to the Church we should define the word a little. We mean the whole Church, the Church as an ecumenical body spread around the world, and not just its particular form in a parish in a local community. The Church we are talking about is a tremendously powerful institution in our society, and in the world. That Church is one form of the Presence of God on Earth, and so naturally it is powerful. It is powerful by definition. It is a powerful moral and spiritual force which cannot be ignored by any movement. Furthermore, it is an organization with tremendous wealth. Since the Church is to be servant to the poor, it is *our* fault if that wealth is not channeled to help the poor in our world.

In a small way we have been able, in the Delano strike, to work together with the Church in such a way as to bring some of its moral and economic power to bear on those who want to maintain the status quo, keeping farm workers in virtual enslavement. In brief, here is what happened in Delano.

Some years ago, when some of us were working with the Community Service Organization, we began to realize the powerful effect which the Church can have on the conscience of the opposition. In scattered instances, in San Jose, Sacramento, Oakland, Los Angeles and other places, priests would speak out loudly and clearly against specific instances of oppression, and in some cases, stand with the people who were being hurt. Furthermore, a small group of priests, Frs. McDonald [McDonnell], McCollough, Duggan and others, began to pinpoint attention on the terrible situation of the farm workers in our state.

At about that same time, we began to run into the California Migrant Ministry in the camps and fields. They were about the only ones there, and a lot of us were very suspicious, since we were Catholics and they were Protestants. However, they had developed a very clear conception of the Church. It was called to serve, to be at the mercy of the poor, and not to try to use them. After a while this made a lot of sense to us, and we began to find ourselves working side by side with them. In fact, it forced us to raise the question why OUR Church was not doing the same. We would ask, "Why do the Protestants come out here and help the people, demand nothing, and give all their time to serving farm workers, while our own parish priests stay in their churches, where only a few people come, and usually feel uncomfortable?"

It was not until some of us moved to Delano and began working to build the National Farm Workers Association that we really saw how far removed from the people the parish Church was. In fact, we could not get any help at all from the priests of Delano. When the strike began, they told us we could not even use the Church's auditorium for the meetings. The farm workers' money helped build that auditorium! But the Protestants were there again, in the form of the California Migrant Ministry, and they began to help in little ways, here and there.

When the strike started in 1965, most of our "friends" forsook us for a while. They ran—or were just too busy to help. But the California Migrant Ministry held a meeting with its staff and decided that the strike was a matter of life or death for farm workers everywhere, and that even if it meant the end of the Migrant Ministry they would turn over their resources to the strikers. The political pressure on the Protestant Churches was tremendous and the Migrant Ministry lost a lot of money. But they stuck it out, and they began to point the way to the rest of the Church. In fact, when 30 of the strikers were arrested for shouting Huelga, 11 ministers went to jail with them. They were in Delano that day at the request of Chris Hartmire, director of the California Migrant Ministry.

Then the workers began to raise the question: "Why ministers? Why not priests? What does the Bishop say?" But the Bishop said nothing. But slowly the pressure of the people grew and grew, until finally we have in Delano a priest sent by the new Bishop, Timothy Manning, who is there to help minister to the needs of farm workers. His name is Father Mark Day and he is the Union's chaplain. *Finally,* our own Catholic Church has decided to recognize that we have our own peculiar needs, just as the growers have theirs.

But outside of the local diocese, the pressure built up on growers to negotiate was tremendous. Though we were not allowed to have our own priest, the power of the ecumenical body of the Church was tremendous. The work of the Church, for example, in the Schenley, Di Giorgio, Perelli-Minetti strikes was fantastic. They applied pressure— and they mediated.

When poor people get involved in a long conflict, such as a strike, or a civil rights drive, and the pressure increases each day, there is a deep need for spiritual advice. Without it we see families crumble, leadership weaken, and hard workers grow tired. And in such a situation the spiritual advice must be given by a *friend,* not by the opposition. What sense does it make to go to Mass on Sunday and reach out for spiritual help, and instead get sermons about the wickedness of your cause? That only drives one to question and to despair. The growers in Delano have their spiritual problems . . . we do not deny that. They have every right to have priests and ministers who serve their needs. BUT WE HAVE DIFFERENT NEEDS, AND SO WE NEEDED A FRIENDLY SPIRITUAL GUIDE. And this is true in every community in this state where the poor face tremendous problems.

But the opposition raises a tremendous howl about this. They don't want us to have our spiritual advisors, friendly to our needs. Why is this? Why indeed except that THERE IS TREMENDOUS SPIRITUAL AND ECONOMIC POWER IN THE CHURCH. The rich know it, and for that reason they choose to keep it from the people.

The leadership of the Mexican-American Community must admit that we have fallen far short in our task of helping provide spiritual guidance for our people. We may say, "I don't feel any such need. I can get along." But that is a poor excuse for not helping provide such help for others. For we can also say, "I don't need any welfare help. I can take care of my own problems." But we are all willing to fight like hell for welfare aid for those who truly need it, who would starve without it. Likewise we may have gotten an education and not care about scholarship money for ourselves, or our children. But we would, we should, fight like hell to see to it that our state provides aid for any child needing it so that he can get the education he desires. LIKEWISE WE CAN SAY WE DON'T NEED THE CHURCH. THAT IS OUR BUSINESS. BUT THERE ARE HUNDREDS OF THOUSANDS OF OUR PEOPLE WHO DESPERATELY NEED SOME HELP FROM THAT POWERFUL INSTITUTION, THE CHURCH, AND WE ARE FOOLISH NOT TO HELP THEM GET IT.

For example, the Catholic Charities agencies of the Catholic Church has millions of dollars earmarked for the poor. But often the money is spent for food baskets for the needy instead of for effective action to eradicate the causes of poverty. The men and women who administer this money sincerely want to help their brothers. It should be our duty to help direct the attention to the basic needs of the Mexican-Americans in our society . . . needs which cannot be satisfied with baskets of food, but rather with effective organizing at the grass roots level.

Therefore, I am calling for Mexican-American groups to stop ignoring this source of power. It is not just our right to appeal to the Church to use its power effectively for the poor, it is our duty to do so. It should be as natural as appealing to government . . . and we do that often enough.

Furthermore, we should be prepared to come to the defense of that priest, rabbi, minister, or layman of the Church, who out of commitment to truth and justice gets into a tight place with his pastor or bishop. It behooves us to stand with that man and help him see his trial through. It is our duty to see to it that his rights of conscience are respected and that no bishop, pastor or other higher body takes that God-given, human right away.

Finally, in a nutshell, what do we want the Church to do? We don't ask for more cathedrals. We don't ask for bigger churches or fine gifts. We ask for its presence with us, beside us, as Christ among us. We ask the Church to *sacrifice with the people* for social change, for justice, and for love of brother. We don't ask for words. We ask for deeds. We don't ask for paternalism. We ask for servanthood.

HELEN CHÁVEZ

Helen Chávez Recalls

1975

In his early years of community and labor organizing, César Chávez; his wife, Helen; and his family often faced harsh financial difficulties. In the brief reminiscence below, Helen reveals how little money the family had when, in midsummer of 1958, they moved to El Rio (just outside Oxnard, California), where Chávez assumed leadership of a new Community Service Organization (CSO) project. Throughout his career, Chávez had to depend on his wife and family for financial and moral support.

When we packed up in San Jose, we were so busy we forgot to go to the bank and get any money. The night before, Cesar had gotten sick and was just burning up with fever. I said, "Let's wait." But we had

Jacques Levy, *Cesar Chavez: Autobiography of La Causa* (New York: W. W. Norton, 1975), 128, 147–48.

everything packed, and he had a house meeting that evening. He said, "No, we have to go."

I don't drive, so he had to. Here we get into our beat-up station wagon loaded with this huge rented trailer with all our belongings in it and the kids, and I just had maybe a few dollars.

We had to stop along the way because he was really burning up with fever, and I got a little something for the kids. Then the car stopped completely. We really didn't know what to do. Somebody stopped and helped us, so we gave them our last two dollars. The kids were hungry, but we didn't have any money to buy any food for them.

Finally after that long trip, stopping all along the way, we got to El Rio. There was this little grocery store, and I told Cesar, "Go ask them if they'll cash a check for us because the kids haven't eaten since this morning."

Well, he said, "No, you go," and I said, "No, you go." Finally he said he would, and he got some milk and stuff.

We went up to the little house we had rented, but it was dark, and there was no electricity. I think we had a flashlight. We just threw a few mattresses on the floor so the kids could sleep. I fed them and put them to bed.

Cesar went up to this meeting, sick as he was.

In this abbreviated recollection, Helen Chávez recalls the circumstances facing the Chávez family when her husband made his momentous decision in March 1962 to leave the CSO and found a new union for farmworkers. Throughout their lives, the Chávez family, as Helen says here, "manage[d] some way as long as one of us was able to work."

Cesar had always talked about organizing farm workers, even before CSO. After all, we were both farm workers, and my parents and his parents and our whole families.

Finally, he just made a decision that that's what he was going to do. He did discuss it and say that it would be a lot of work and a lot of sacrifice because we wouldn't have any income coming in. But it didn't worry me. It didn't frighten me. I figured we'd manage some way as long as one of us was able to work.

I never had any doubts that he would succeed. I thought a lot of people felt the way we did.

The Reverend James Drake Recalls

1975

The Reverend James Drake, one of the coterie of Protestant ministers and reformers who aided Chávez in the 1950s and 1960s, remembers in this selection important ingredients of Chávez's new farmworker organization in the 1960s. Chávez raised his own funds; won supporters by careful, one-on-one contacts; and provided food and clothing, as well as encouragement, for needy Mexican Americans. What Drake saw in the 1960s became trademarks of Chávez's organizational tactics and humanitarian efforts throughout his career.

I really thought Cesar was crazy. Everybody did except Helen. They had so many children and so little to eat, and that old 1953 Mercury station wagon gobbled up gas and oil. Everything he wanted to do seemed impossible. He used his tiny garage as his headquarters, but it was so hot in there, all the ink melted down in the mimeograph machine I lent him.

What impressed me was that even though Cesar was desperate, he didn't want our money, or Teamster money, or AFL-CIO money, or any other money that might compromise him. Right from the start, he made it clear that his organization would be independent. And I was impressed by his perseverance. Building the union was a slow, plodding thing based on hard work and very personal relationships. The growers didn't know he was in town, but the workers knew. After a while, they were coming to his house day and night for help.

The National Farm Workers Association did not just happen. Its development, like everything the Chavez family approached, was mapped out with a design toward success. Workers were not organized in dramatic meetings, but one by one, in a car on the way to a labor commissioner hearing, or while driving to meet an industrial accident referee. And while the new member drove, Cesar talked. He talked clearly and carefully, and the plan was set forth. The trips were

Jacques Levy, *Cesar Chavez: Autobiography of La Causa* (New York: W. W. Norton, 1975), 162–63.

not futile either, for a growing number of farm workers passed the word, "If you have trouble, go to Delano. Chavez can help."

Tragedy strikes farm workers in the same ways that it does other families, but there has seldom been a place for a farm worker family to turn. In the NFWA, a knock in the middle of the night at the Chavez home could often materialize quick help. The pains taken by Cesar were never part of an act. They were a very real extension of his philosophy that human beings are subjects to be taken seriously.

DOLORES HUERTA

Dolores Huerta Recalls

1975

Dolores Huerta, Chávez's most notable colleague, illuminates the spiritual qualities of his leadership in this recollection. In mid-February 1968, Chávez began a twenty-five-day fast to refocus himself and his followers on the need for unity and for nonviolent action. Huerta also points up the difficulties that Chávez's liberal, secular supporters had in understanding and affirming the religious and moral bent to his thinking and actions.

We arrived in New York about January 20, and Cesar went on the fast February 15. We all got hit with it suddenly, because he didn't tell anybody until he had been fasting for about five days. When I heard about it, I vomited, and I know the women on the boycott in New York broke down and started crying. I think I lost eight pounds the first week of his fast. All of us understood the religious aspect of it, so we had a priest come over from Brooklyn the next Sunday and give us this special mass.

Fred [Ross] reacted very strongly, too, because I think Fred probably loves Cesar more than anybody in the world—maybe even more than his wife and children.

Jacques Levy, *Cesar Chavez: Autobiography of La Causa* (New York: W. W. Norton, 1975), 277–78.

Some people reacted the other way, they just missed the whole point of the thing. A lot of people thought Cesar was trying to play God, that this guy really was trying to pull a saintly act.

Poor Cesar! They just couldn't accept it for what it was. I know it's hard for people who are not Mexican to understand, but this is part of the Mexican culture—the penance, the whole idea of suffering for something, of self-inflicted punishment. It's a tradition of very long standing. In fact, Cesar has often mentioned in speeches that we will not win through violence, we will win through fasting and prayer.

I wasn't in Delano at all during the fast, but a lot of unpleasant things happened there at that time in terms of the organization. Tony Orendain, who was the secretary-treasurer of the Union, was very cynical against the church. He was one of the guys that was a leader in all of the conflicts that took place when Cesar went on the fast. There's an awful lot of bigotry even among Mexicans, especially the ones from Mexico.

But the reaction was widespread. Sometime after the fast started, Fred and I were talking on the phone to Saul Alinsky, who said he had told Cesar how embarrassing it was to the Industrial Areas Foundation for Cesar to go on that fast.

And I said, "Well, you should be glad that he didn't do it while he was still working for you."

Alinsky said, "We've had a terrible time trying to explain it."

And then Fred—you just can't say anything against Cesar without Fred reacting—said, "Yea, Saul, but you don't know what a good organizing technique that was, because by that fast he was able to unify the farm workers all over the state of California. Prior to that fast, there had been a lot of bickering and backbiting and fighting and little attempts at violence. But Cesar brought everybody together and really established himself as the leader of the farm workers."

And Saul was at a loss for words.

But that was the reaction of many liberals and radicals. Cesar feels that liberals are liberal right up to the steps of the Catholic church. Guys can be liberal about homosexuality, about dope, about capital punishment, about everything but the Catholic church. There the liberalism ends. So he doesn't want to feed the bigotry that the average person has against the church. He tries to overcome that bigotry by his example.

JACQUES LEVY

From Jacques Levy's Notebook

1975

The next three selections, all from Jacques Levy's "notebook," describe Chávez's intensity, his jail experiences, and his commitment to nonviolence. These recollections from 1969, 1970, and 1973, respectively, are drawn from Levy's book Cesar Chavez: Autobiography of La Causa, *the best firsthand source on Chávez and the farmworkers. Levy frequently traveled with Chávez, recorded and edited their conversations, and gathered reminiscences from Chávez's chief lieutenants. This trio of excerpts reveals much about the personal side of Chávez.*

February 6, 1969—From early morning to late at night, Cesar handles union business from his bed, holding meeting after meeting. It is his regular routine. His face is drawn with fatigue and etched with pain. During our interview, I ask him about his sudden incapacitation, about the severe muscle spasms which are the result of a lifetime of trying to compensate for the unequal length of his legs.

"At first I counted the days without pain," he says, "but as I got better, I started counting the days with pain."

His office is a tiny bedroom filled with a large hospital bed and a standing blackboard. The walls are orange-pink, his electric blanket a deep orange. To the right, behind his bed are a wooden crucifix and a photograph of a Bufano* statue of St. Francis; on the right wall, a huge picture of Gandhi, a smaller portrait of Robert Kennedy, and a woodcut of a family bur[y]ing their dead. Behind his bed, to the left, there is a black poster featuring three heads—those of President John Kennedy, Martin Luther King, Jr., and Senator Robert Kennedy—and one word in red letters—"WHY?" There is also a small cloth hanging with the word "Love."

The spirit of martyrs fills the room....

* * *

*Sculptor and artist Beniamino ("Benny") Bufano (1898–1970)

Jacques Levy, *Cesar Chavez: Autobiography of La Causa* (New York: W. W. Norton, 1975), 293, 429–30, 489–90.

It is damp, dark, and foggy when the vigil starts in the parking lot across the street from the jail, the day Cesar is locked up.

Some three dozen votive candles flicker in a makeshift shrine in the back of a rented pickup. The candles throw a soft light on the gold and brown Virgin of Guadalupe, flanked by flowers. The altar is draped with black cloth and decorated with the American, Mexican, and union flags. Tinsel borders the black cloth, and a small banner with Viva Chavez is pinned on it.

Alongside the truck, several dozen farm workers vow the vigil will last as long as Cesar remains in jail. One of them, Modesto Negrete, a tomato picker from King City, pledges to fast for the duration.

The next day, a woman drives up to the shrine and starts talking to one of the workers. She tells how she was against the Cause because she thought the people were dirty, and she was outraged by the union's red flag and the strike.

But, she says, she was at the courthouse yesterday and saw one of the farm workers put out his cigarette on the floor. Then another worker came up to him and told him it was wrong. So the first worker picked up the butt and put it in his pocket.

The lady says she was deeply moved by that and the workers' behavior, and she wants to give five dollars to the Cause.

The worker thanks her and asks for her name and address[,] so the union can send her a thank you letter.

No, the lady says. She wants to remain anonymous.

"Why?"

"My son is a grower.". . .

June 8, 1973—The Teamsters put on a show for the TV cameras, pulling workers out of the field to wave blue Teamster flags along the edge of the vineyard facing the UFW picket line.

Both sides soon are yelling at each other, exchanging taunts and slurs.

Later, Cesar chews out the picket captains. "For the first time I saw a lot of hate," he tells them. "You've got to go back and work with those people."

The picket lines should not insult the scabs, he says. That just pushes them into the Teamster camp. "If we had elections, we'd lose them today. We would have won them yesterday."

He urges the picket captains to win the workers over if they leave their work to face the UFW lines.

STUDS TERKEL

César Chávez

1970

When famed oral historian Studs Terkel interviewed Chávez in the late 1960s, Chávez provided revealing remembrances about the dislocations he and his parents had felt in losing their land in Arizona and being forced to become field workers. He recalled new insecurities, the loss of pride, and prejudices he had experienced as a boy and a young man. These early, powerful memories help to explain his later motivation and commitment in leading his beloved Mexican American farmworkers.

Oh, I remember having to move out of our house. My father had brought in a team of horses and wagon. We had always lived in that house, and we couldn't understand why we were moving out. When we got to the other house, it was a worse house, a poor house. That must have been around 1934. I was about six years old.

It's known as the North Gila Valley, about fifty miles north of Yuma. My dad was being turned out of his small plot of land. He had inherited this from his father, who had homesteaded it. I saw my two, three other uncles also moving out. And for the same reason. The bank had foreclosed on the loan.

If the local bank approved, the Government would guarantee the loan and small farmers like my father would continue in business. It so happened the president of the bank was the guy who most wanted our land. We were surrounded by him: he owned all the land around us. Of course, he wouldn't pass the loan.

One morning a giant tractor came in, like we had never seen before. My daddy used to do all his work with horses. So this huge tractor came in and began to knock down this corral, this small corral where my father kept his horses. We didn't understand why. In the matter of a week, the whole face of the land was changed. Ditches were dug, and it was different. I didn't like it as much.

We all of us climbed into an old Chevy that my dad had. And then we were in California, and migratory workers. There were five kids—

Studs Terkel, "Cesar Chavez," in *Hard Times: An Oral History of the Great Depression* (New York: Pantheon Books, 1970), 58–62.

a small family by those standards. It must have been around '36. I was about eight. Well, it was a strange life. We had been poor, but we knew every night there was a bed *there,* and that *this* was our room. There was a kitchen. It was sort of a settled life, and we had chickens and hogs, eggs and all those things. But that all of a sudden changed. When you're small, you can't figure these things out. You know something's not right and you don't like it, but you don't question it and you don't let that get you down. You sort of just continue to move.

But this had quite an impact on my father. He had been used to owning the land and all of a sudden there was no more land. What I heard . . . what I made out of conversations between my mother and my father—things like, we'll work this season and then we'll get enough money and we'll go and buy a piece of land in Arizona. Things like that. Became like a habit. He never gave up hope that someday he would come back and get a little piece of land.

I can understand very, very well this feeling. These conversations were sort of melancholy. I guess my brothers and my sisters could also see this very sad look on my father's face.

That piece of land he wanted . . . ?

No, never. It never happened. He stopped talking about that some years ago. The drive for land, it's a very powerful drive.

When we moved to California, we would work after school. Sometimes we wouldn't go. "Following the crops," we missed much school. Trying to get enough money to stay alive the following winter, the whole family picking apricots, walnuts, prunes. We were pretty new, we had never been migratory workers. We were taken advantage of quite a bit by the labor contractor and the crew pusher.[1] In some pretty silly ways. (Laughs.)

Sometimes we can't help but laugh about it. We trusted everybody that came around. You're traveling in California with all your belongings in your car: it's obvious. Those days we didn't have a trailer. This is bait for the labor contractor. Anywhere we stopped, there was a labor contractor offering all kinds of jobs and good wages, and we were always deceived by them and we always went. Trust them.

Coming into San Jose, not finding—being lied to, that there was work. We had no money at all, and had to live on the outskirts of town under a bridge and dry creek. That wasn't really unbearable. What

---

[1] "That's a man who specializes in contracting human beings to do cheap labor."

was unbearable was so many families living just a quarter of a mile. And you know how kids are. They'd bring in those things that really hurt us quite a bit. Most of those kids were middle-class families.

We got hooked on a real scheme once. We were going by Fresno on our way to Delano. We stopped at some service station and this labor contractor saw the car. He offered a lot of money. We went. We worked the first week: the grapes were pretty bad and we couldn't make much. We all stayed off from school in order to make some money. Saturday we were to be paid and we didn't get paid. He came and said the winery hadn't paid him. We'd have money next week. He gave us $10. My dad took the $10 and went to the store and bought $10 worth of groceries. So we worked another week and in the middle of the second week, my father was asking him for his last week's pay, and he had the same excuse. This went on and we'd get $5 or $10 or $7 a week for about four weeks. For the whole family.

So one morning my father made the resolution no more work. If he doesn't pay us, we won't work. We got in a car and went over to see him. The house was empty. He had left. The winery said they had paid him and they showed us where they had paid him. This man had taken it.

Labor strikes were everywhere. We were one of the strikingest families, I guess. My dad didn't like the conditions, and he began to agitate. Some families would follow, and we'd go elsewhere. Sometimes we'd come back. We couldn't find a job elsewhere, so we'd come back. Sort of beg for a job. Employers would know and they would make it very humiliating. . . .

Did these strikes ever win?

Never.

We were among these families who always honored somebody else's grievance. Somebody would have a personal grievance with the employer. He'd say I'm not gonna work for this man. Even though we were working, we'd honor it. We felt we had to. So we'd walk out, too. Because we were prepared to honor those things, we caused many of the things ourselves. If we were picking at a piece rate and we knew they were cheating on the weight, we wouldn't stand for it. So we'd lose the job, and we'd go elsewhere. There were other families like that.

Sometimes when you had to come back, the contractor knew this. . . ?

*   *   *

They knew it, and they rubbed it in quite well. Sort of shameful to come back. We were trapped. We'd have to do it for a few days to get enough money to get enough gas.

One of the experiences I had. We went through Indio, California. Along the highway there were signs in most of the small restaurants that said "White Trade Only." My dad read English, but he didn't really know the meaning. He went in to get some coffee—a pot that he had, to get some coffee for my mother. He asked us not to come in, but we followed him anyway. And this young waitress said, "We don't serve Mexicans here. Get out of here." I was there, and I saw it and heard it. She paid no more attention. I'm sure for the rest of her life she never thought of it again. But every time we thought of it, it hurt us. So we got back in the car and we had a difficult time trying—in fact, we never got the coffee. These are sort of unimportant, but they're . . . you remember 'em very well.

One time there was a little diner across the tracks in Brawley. We used to shine shoes after school. Saturday was a good day. We used to shine shoes for three cents, two cents. Hamburgers were then, as I remember, seven cents. There was this little diner all the way across town. The moment we stepped across the tracks, the police stopped us. They would let us go there, to what we called "the American town," the Anglo town, with a shoe shine box. We went to this little place and we walked in.

There was this young waitress again. With either her boyfriend or someone close, because they were involved in conversation. And there was this familiar sign again, but we paid no attention to it. She looked up at us and she sort of—it wasn't what she said, it was just a gesture. A sort of gesture of total rejection. Her hand, you know, and the way she turned her face away from us. She said: "Wattaya want?" So we told her we'd like to buy two hamburgers. She sort of laughed, a sarcastic sort of laugh. And she said, "Oh, we don't sell to Mexicans. Why don't you go across to Mexican town, you can buy 'em over there." And then she turned around and continued her conversation.

She never knew how much she was hurting us. But it stayed with us.

We'd go to school two days sometimes, a week, two weeks, three weeks at most. This is when we were migrating. We'd come back to our winter base, and if we were lucky, we'd get in a good solid all of January, February, March, April, May. So we had five months out of a possible nine months. We started counting how many schools we'd been to and we counted thirty-seven. Elementary schools. From first to eighth grade. Thirty-seven. We never got a transfer. Friday we didn't tell the teacher or anything. We'd just go home. And they accepted this.

I remember one teacher—I wondered why she was asking so many questions. (In those days anybody asked questions, you became suspicious. Either a cop or a social worker.) She was a young teacher, and she just wanted to know why we were behind. One day she drove into the camp. That was quite an event, because we never had a teacher come over. Never. So it was, you know, a very meaningful day for us.

This I remember. Some people put this out of their minds and forget it. I don't. I don't want to forget it. I don't want it to take the best of me, but I want to be there because this is what happened. This is the truth, you know. History.

JACK KING

Chávez and the UFW:
A View from the California Farm Bureau

1979

Chief among Chávez's critics were large growers and the California Farm Bureau Federation. In this editorial distributed to California newspapers in 1979, Jack King, a spokesman for the Farm Bureau, censured Chávez for his unyielding "ideology," his "demands," and his "rigidity and pressure tactics." King was attacking Chávez for launching a boycott against SunHarvest, where union workers were striking.

Cesar Chavez has termed the current California farmworker strike a "dream come true." But it's a view which may not be as widely shared among rank and file UFW members as their leader would like to believe. There are signs of growing uneasiness among the members

---

Jack King, "Chavez and the UFW: A View from the California Farm Bureau," in Susan Ferriss and Ricardo Sandoval, *The Fight in the Fields: Cesar Chavez and the Farmworkers Movement* (New York: Harcourt Brace, 1997), 196.

of the strike-idled union as the weeks turn into months with no sign of progress in the negotiations.

A federal observer to the talks reports there appears to be little interest on the part of the UFW to engage in serious negotiation. A regional director of the Agricultural Labor Relations Board admits he has no idea what the real motives of the union are. Some things are readily apparent: lettuce is rotting in the fields, more than four thousand farmworkers are out of work, and tensions are building.

Employer representatives have asked for federal mediation but the UFW refuses. Shunning the negotiations, Chavez instead is turning to his most familiar weapon—a national boycott. The target is Chiquita bananas marketed by United Brands, a parent company of Sun-Harvest, one of the struck companies. Through the use of the boycott, Chavez hopes to drum up public appeal, his strongest suit to compensate for his biggest weakness—a reasonable bargaining position.

When the California Agricultural Labor Relations Act became law in 1976, most observers felt the farm labor situation would stabilize and be marked by hard bargaining on both sides. With the capitulation of the Teamsters, the way seemed clear for the UFW to write impressive new labor contracts. Labor experts predicted it would be a time of maturation for the UFW during which they would develop their skills as seasoned contract negotiators.

But anyone who had negotiated an earlier contract with Chavez knew the transition would not come easy. Chavez doesn't negotiate; he demands. Guided by a master plan based on his ideology, Chavez pays little heed to the basis of labor relations compromise. And while the Teamsters are known for their business acumen and shrewd negotiating, the UFW is better known for its rigidity and pressure tactics. Whereas the Teamsters union knows that its future depends on the viability of the company it deals with, Chavez would seem to care less.

To the UFW leadership, the heart of the union is still the "cause." For Chavez it is far more gratifying to spread the gospel than to engage in prolonged negotiating sessions and mundane organizational matters.

ALLAN GRANT

California Farm Bureau President Recalls

1975

Another opponent, Allan Grant, also of the California Farm Bureau Federation, likewise spoke against Chávez's boycott tactics. Grant argued that previously growers "had gotten along with unions" but that Chávez's farmworkers had disrupted these alleged cordial relations. The violence, destruction of property, and interunion rivalries were, according to Grant, the negative consequences of Chávez's boycotts. This recollection, recalling events of the mid-1970s, illustrates the strong antipathy that growers, businessmen, and conservative politicians held for Chávez and the United Farm Workers.

We were trying for twelve years to get farm labor legislation. I started working on this before Governor Ronald Reagan was elected. Therefore, we were very pleased that Governor [Jerry] Brown saw fit to work so hard on it. He could do some things that the former governor couldn't do, because he is a Democrat, and he had a Democratic legislature.

All the farm organizations supported the governor's bill, with the exception of one or two. The boycott was only a minor reason. It did affect us. It put a lot of small grape growers out of business, and it had some effect in lettuce. But more important was the violence that took place, the property destruction, and the very strong antipathy felt between the two unions.

The growers had gotten along with unions for several years, and they're just the same as any other employer. They could adjust to whatever situation comes along, and costs would have to be passed on to the consumer.

Jacques Levy, *Cesar Chavez: Autobiography of La Causa* (New York: W. W. Norton, 1975), 533–34.

PART THREE

An Illustrated Life

César Chávez and His Times in Photographs

Visual images are an important part of history. Photographs and other representational sources help students to picture people and to understand their social and physical settings. Any revealing biographical study must take advantage of the power that visual images impart to readers.

This collection of photographs provides a selective, illustrated life of César Chávez. Images of Chávez's family and his colleagues, photographs of the labor activities of Chávez and his followers, and pictures of other aspects of his life add immeasurably to an understanding of his career. Chávez himself understood and used the power of visual images. Something of a camera buff, he enjoyed snapping posed as well as candid pictures of his friends, followers, and labor gatherings.

These photographs dramatize the private and public sides of Chávez. Accompanying the photographs are narrative and interpretive captions to draw readers into the reprinted images. The questions that preface these illustrations will help students ponder the meaning of these visual images.

Questions for Consideration

1. If you had only these visual images with which to interpret César Chávez, what could you conclude about him?

2. What are the predominant themes depicted in these photo-graphs?
3. What can you understand about Chávez's religious ideas from these images?
4. Which photographs seem the most posed? Do any seem contrived or phony?
5. Select what you consider to be the two most revealing photographs in this collection. Why are they the most revealing?

Chávez thought a lot about his family and the families of his supporters. In his eyes, family and moral values were intertwined, so he often worried that his time-consuming commitments to the farmworkers would distract him from his growing family. His wife, Helen, preferred to stay at home with their children, although early in his labor-organizing career, she worked in the fields to help support the family. Later, several of the Chávez children became active in UFW activities. César and Helen Chávez posed for this photo with six of their eight children in the early 1960s.
Walter P. Reuther Library, Wayne State University.

Throughout his career, Chávez linked his religious devotion and his labor activism. Religious symbols were nearly always present at his meetings, marches, and fasts. Although Chávez had no difficulty linking his spirituality and his farmworker activities, some of his followers did. Some supported his ties to religious groups—Catholic, Protestant, and Jewish; but others, more interested in Chávez's field worker organizations and other liberal causes, disliked his explicit uses of spiritual symbols. Chávez's identification with both religious and secular symbols is clear in this photograph with the statues of the Virgin of Guadalupe overlooking and protecting copies of the UFW newspaper, *El Malcriado.*

Reproduction by Timothy Moy.

Chávez worked long hours trying to support his family and to hold the farmworkers together and keep them committed to nonviolence. Even after he organized the FWA in 1962, he often arose at four or five in the morning to work in the fields. Later, he maintained equally long days, working until midnight or later on union matters. His supporters praised his tireless and selfless efforts, but his critics sometimes accused him of arbitrary decisions and selfish acts. Some critics also asserted that Chávez suffered from a martyr complex. Obviously leadership and its demands were difficult for Chávez.

Walter P. Reuther Library, Wayne State University.

Like Chávez's marches, his fasts often combined religious commitment, a focus on nonviolence, and an understanding of the value and
use of media publicity. This wonderfully emblematic photograph
shows Chávez breaking bread at the end of a fast in 1968 with Robert
Kennedy, then an unannounced but leading Democratic presidential
candidate. To Chávez's left is his mother, Juana, and to his right,
beyond Kennedy, is his wife, Helen. Behind him are farmworkers and
union colleagues.

Walter P. Reuther Library, Wayne State University.

Throughout his public career, César Chávez exhibited a large interest in the use of symbols. This interest displayed itself in his marches, fasts, and religious observances. When he spoke at labor rallies, he often stood with union and patriotic symbols. This photo captures one such occasion. The UFW and American flags were two symbols Chávez often utilized, but on other occasions he effectively used religious and Mexican symbols.

Walter P. Reuther Library, Wayne State University.

On July 29, 1970, a euphoric Chávez signed contracts with several leading grape growers to end the five-year Delano strike. Consider the configuration of this photo. To Chávez's left is John Giumarra, a well-known grower, whose upraised hands seem to signal resignation as much as agreement. Behind Chávez and Giumarra are two Catholic priests and the editor of the *Catholic Monitor.* On the back wall are both labor and religious symbols.

Walter P. Reuther Library, Wayne State University.

From the 1960s on, Dolores Huerta was a stalwart lieutenant in Chávez's cause. Although they sometimes strongly disagreed about tactics, they were united on most farmworker goals. Occasionally, Chávez would question Huerta about paying too little attention to her large family (she had eleven children), but he also valued, praised, and depended on her leadership talents and superb skills as a labor negotiator.

Walter P. Reuther Library, Wayne State University.

A variety of religious activists—Catholic, Protestant, Jewish, and others—supported Chávez and his farmworkers. The noted Catholic reformer Dorothy Day, editor of the *Catholic Worker,* aided Chávez in several ways. She not only wrote supportive editorials about his activities and organizations, she traveled from New York City, despite her advancing age and frail health, to join the farmworker picket lines. A lifelong advocate of urban and agricultural workers, she was convinced that Christians must move out from their churches into the streets and fields to help laborers. Later, she encouraged and helped fund César and Helen Chávez's trip to Europe to visit Pope Paul VI. Walter P. Reuther Library, Wayne State University.

During the fall of 1974, César, Helen, and their son-in-law took a three-week trip abroad to help expand the boycott of grapes being dumped in Europe after not selling in the United States and Canada. The trip also was part of Chávez's efforts to enlarge his support among international religious and labor organizations. When he refused to allow the UFW to pay his travel expenses, other American labor and religious groups funded the trip. While in Europe, César and Helen were granted a private audience in Rome with Pope Paul VI on September 25. The Pope praised Chávez for applying Christian principles to his social justice efforts for field workers. The pontiff also lauded Chávez's "spirit of cooperation," and his endeavors to preserve harmony, understanding, and "liberty and justice for all." Chávez recalled the visit with Pope Paul as "one of the highlights" of his life. It was "like a small miracle" for him, as a Roman Catholic, to "see the Holy Father in person."

Walter P. Reuther Library, Wayne State University.

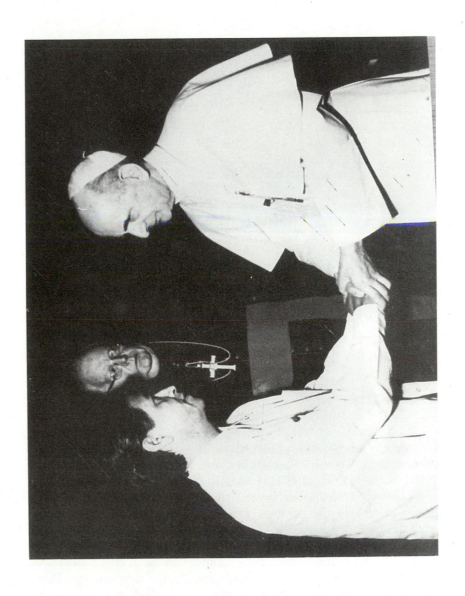

Chávez encouraged the participation of El Teatro Campesino (The Farmworkers Theater) in marches and union rallies. Begun in the 1960s as the brainchild of Luís Valdez, the field worker drama group entertained American, European, and Latin American audiences with its brand of bilingual humour. The group performed its skits, often from the back of a flatbed truck, to raise the spirits of workers and to clarify the inequities laborers experienced. Usually, growers or labor contractors were the butt of performances by El Teatro Campesino, but on occasion the actors also poked fun at naïve farmworkers. Here, "Don Coyote," a labor contractor, attempts to ride on the back of a bucking field worker.

Walter P. Reuther Library, Wayne State University.

PART FOUR

A Life and
Its Interpreters

Historians often use the word *historiography*. In their application of the word, some scholars refer to the varied research techniques historians use. Others mean the dissimilar and often changing interpretations of important historical persons, events, and ideas. This part illustrates the second meaning of historiography.

There is a historiography of César Chávez. That is, over time, authors have presented conflicting images of Chávez, and their interpretations have frequently changed. For example, in the first two selections here, notice Fred Ross's very positive reminiscences of Chávez as a beginning labor organizer. Consider, too, the high regard for Chávez that Martin Luther King Jr. reveals in his brief telegram.

The next two examples of this evolving historiography come from the work of two professional historians writing after Chávez's death in 1993. Richard Griswold del Castillo, coauthor of the best biography of Chávez and a leading Chicano historian, provides a sympathetic overview of Chávez's role in the early months of the Delano strike. In the next essay, Margaret Rose, *the* specialist on women's roles in the UFW, furnishes another perspective by examining Dolores Huerta's reactions to and evaluations of Chávez.

The final two selections present opposite conclusions about Chávez. Frank Bardacke is critical of Chávez in his essay "César's Ghost," whereas Peter Matthiessen, author of a well-received book on

Chávez, *Sal Si Puedes,* praises him as a memorable "spiritual" and reform leader in late-twentieth-century America.

Students should examine and weigh carefully these changing and differing interpretations of Chávez as they come to their own conclusions about him.

Questions for Consideration

1. What positive characteristics did labor organizer Fred Ross see in his early contacts with César Chávez?
2. What are your reactions to the words that Martin Luther King Jr. used in his telegram to Chávez?
3. What kind of Chávez emerges from Richard Griswold del Castillo's "The Birth of La Causa"?
4. Which of Chávez's qualities appealed most to Dolores Huerta?
5. Do you agree with Frank Bardacke's criticisms of Chávez? Which criticism do you find the most persuasive? The least convincing?
6. Peter Matthiessen praises Chávez's spiritual, mystical, and self-sacrificing natures. Which of these strengths do you consider the most important in understanding Chávez the man?

FRED ROSS

Fred Ross Recalls

1975

Fred Ross was a key figure in Chávez's early efforts as a labor organizer. Notice in the first, and more extensive, reminiscence how positively Ross recalls Chávez's quick and enthusiastic participation in organizational efforts. The portraits that Ross paints in these two profiles replicate what most early observers said about Chávez: He was tireless, devoted to his causes, and willing to outwork any of his colleagues. These snapshot glimpses of the man in the late 1940s and early 1950s prefigured the very positive interpretations of him that emerged in his first years of organizational work.

Jacques Levy, *Cesar Chavez: Autobiography of La Causa* (New York: W. W. Norton, 1975), 99–102, 112–13.

I was born in San Francisco in 1910, so when I met Cesar I was barely forty-two, and I only had six years of organizing behind me. All that I had organized then was the Los Angeles CSO. That gives Cesar encouragement. He says, "Look what Fred Ross did after he was forty-two." By the time Cesar was forty-two, he had seventeen years of experience organizing.

I didn't start out to be an organizer[.] I graduated from Southern California with a general secondary teaching credential in 1936, but it was the depression, and I couldn't get a job. In 1937 I got a job with the state relief administration as a caseworker, in effect a social worker.

Then I quit and went to work for the Farm Security Administration, a federal job, in charge of their relief program in the Coachella Valley. They had a warehouse with commodities to give out, flour, beans, and such.

The next year I was put in charge of the federal farm labor camp at Arvin. That was the camp written up by John Steinbeck in *Grapes of Wrath,* the one the Joad family went to, but he finished his book before I got there. Later I was promoted to assistant chief of community services covering some twenty-five camps in California and Arizona.

When the war started in December 1941, my boss called and told me that from now on, "We must work with the growers, and you don't have enough petty larceny in your heart to do that." So I went to work for the War Relocation Authority.

After the war I worked for the American Council of Race Relations, a Chicago-based organization, and went down to San Bernardino to help set up Councils for Civic Unity. Our goal was to create unity, and end the riots then going on between whites and minorities.

In Chicago, the well-known organizer, Saul Alinsky, used to play pinochle with Louis Wirth, the director of the American Council of Race Relations, who didn't like my work. He told Alinsky he had sent me down to make a survey, but that I was organizing people. "That's not why we sent him," he said.

Alinsky's ears pricked up. He was head of the Industrial Areas Foundation, which was doing community organizing in the Chicago slums, and he was looking for organizers. Alinsky hired me in September of 1947 to begin organizing Mexican-Americans in Los Angeles, as that was the hub of the whole Mexican-American population.

I'd been organizing for about six years in Southern California, five of those for the Industrial Areas Foundation, when I came north to San Jose, the largest Spanish center outside of Los Angeles.

It's been written many times that Saul Alinsky trained me and Cesar, but it's not true. I'd been at it over a year before I met him. I was the one who developed the house-meeting technique we used in CSO, and that developed in a kind of evolutionary way.

Of course, at the beginning, I didn't know anything as far as setting up a mass-based organization. I had never done it. But house meetings worked. Cesar later used the house-meeting technique to start the Union.

First I'd hold small house meetings for three weeks, building up to the big organizing meeting when we'd set up temporary officers. Then we'd organize through house meetings for several more weeks before the second organizing meeting. We then would have a working CSO chapter.

From the beginning in 1946, when I was working in the citrus belt, voter registration was the big thing we hit hard. That emphasis evolved, too. At first I couldn't figure out why there was no organization among Mexican-Americans, and why they were clear down at the bottom of the heap. Then about the second unity group I started, I got just a little hint of why.

They were fighting a segregated school case. The Mexican and black kids were going to one school, and the Anglo kids were picked up by bus and taken to another school. It was in Riverside County, a place called Belltown.

A bond election was coming up to fix up the good school, but there was not one cent for the horrible school. So the Chicanos didn't want those bonds to pass. Then they found out none were registered to vote.

As soon as a member of the NAACP started registering people and turned in a registration book, there was a difference. Since bond elections needed a two-thirds vote to pass, the school board saw they might have enough votes in the barrio to kill this bond if they joined with those people in the rest of the community who didn't want to pay any more taxes.

Later I went over to Riverside itself, the Casa Blanca barrio. An orange grower supposedly represented Casa Blanca on the city council, but always refused to come out there because the Casa Blanca people had gone on strike against him.

The Casa Blanca people were pretty anxious to dump him, and from the little I learned in Belltown, I got the idea of the balance of power. If the people all threw their weight one way, that's the way the election would go.

That was the first time I actually went down to the voter registrar and counted those registered with Spanish surnames. There were less than 10 percent in those particular precincts.

That was in 1946. It worked. I got the people registered in Casa Blanca, and they threw the orange grower out. They voted single shot—all voting for the opponent. If they had split their vote, the incumbent would have won. That was the first time I saw it work on a candidate.

As for Belltown, they gave in on the segregated school, integrated the schools, and the school bonds passed. So that set the pattern as far as my type of organization was concerned. I had all the proof I needed.

Later in CSO there were two broad-based programs we did wherever we went—voter registration and citizenship classes. We never left a place until we had put on both of those power-building programs.

I'd been working in San Jose over three weeks, and we'd already had the first organizing meeting before I met Cesar. I remember he was interested in what was in it for farm workers. That first house meeting on June 9 lasted about two hours. Just before I broke away I said I had another meeting at the Flores place. Cesar volunteered to show me the way.

Well, he was hooked. He wanted to move on and see how other people reacted. Although he was still but a semiparticipant, at least he saw the way people would open up at a house meeting, especially when the meeting was relatively small so that they could open up without being embarrassed to say what was on their minds about their problems and the neighborhood.

The night after I met Cesar, we were going to start on the voter registration drive, and he volunteered right away. That was another proof of his interest. We only had one deputy registrar then, and I'd already gotten fifteen to seventeen persons to act as bird dogs going up and down the street pulling the people out to go down to the corner and register. Cesar said he would be there the next night, and he was.

At the very first meeting, I was very much impressed with Cesar. I could tell he was intensely interested, a kind of burning interest rather than one of those inflammatory things that lasts one night and is then forgotten. He asked many questions, part of it to see if I really knew, putting me to the test. But it was much more than that.

He understood it almost immediately, as soon as I drew the picture.

He got the point—the whole question of power and the development of power within the group. He made the connections very quickly between the civic weakness of the group and the social neglect in the barrio, and also conversely, what could be done about that social neglect once the power was developed.

He also showed tremendous perseverance right from the very beginning. Although Helen was quite sick at the time with a kidney disorder, he was the only one in the whole organization that came out every night for two months to push that voter registration drive. For whatever reason, all of his actions were invested with a tremendous amount of urgency.

He felt pretty hurt, I remember, when others started falling by the wayside, people that started out with him, that we had high hopes for.

I kept a diary in those days. And the first night I met Cesar, I wrote in it, "I think I've found the guy I'm looking for." It was obvious even then. . . .

As Cesar was out of work, I talked to Alinsky to see if he couldn't possibly get some money to hire him. Cesar was very modest about his abilities and frightened that he might not be able to do the job. But I talked him into coming on and assigned him to finish the work I had started in Decoto (what is now Union City in Southern Alameda County) while I moved on to the Salinas Valley. It was tough following in my footsteps, as he had to show them he wasn't just a young, dumb kid. He was very young then, only twenty-five, and looked younger, while I was nearly forty-three.

He learned how to skirt around the opposition to him. One of his little techniques has always been to shame people into doing something by letting them know how hard he and others were working, and how it was going to hurt other people if they didn't help too. I think that was one of the things he learned there.

So Decoto was his baptism, but he wanted to get into a place where he didn't have to follow anybody. Some way he fixed it with a priest, Father Gerald Cox, so that he would be invited to go into Oakland to start a voter registration drive. Of course, he became so indispensable that he really had to stay to organize a CSO chapter. It was really there that he proved himself to himself.

MARTIN LUTHER KING JR.

Telegram

September 22, 1966

In this telegram, Martin Luther King Jr. revealed his strong regard for Chávez and his leadership of the farmworkers. King was congratulating Chávez for a victory the National Farm Workers Association had just won over the Teamsters to unionize the field workers. King struck a note familiar to his own listeners in writing to Chávez about their mutual "dreams for a better tomorrow." Chávez watched carefully and learned from King's use of nonviolent tactics. King's endorsement of Chávez also illustrates the early positive interpretations of his work.

As brothers in the fight for equality, I extend the hand of fellowship and good will and wish continuing success to you and your members. The fight for equality must be fought on many fronts—in the urban slums, in the sweat shops of the factories and fields. Our separate struggles are really one—a struggle for freedom, for dignity, and for humanity. You and your valiant fellow workers have demonstrated your commitment to righting grievous wrongs forced upon exploited people. We are together with you in spirit and in determination that our dreams for a better tomorrow will be realized.

Jacques Levy, *Cesar Chavez: Autobiography of La Causa* (New York: W. W. Norton, 1975), 246.

The Birth of La Causa

1995

This account of Chávez's launching of the notable strike in Delano, California, in 1965 places his efforts in the context of the yeasty 1960s. A leading Chicano historian, Griswold del Castillo agrees with the sympathetic historical and biographical treatments of Chávez that appeared earlier in the 1970s and 1980s. But this chapter, taken from the best biography of Chávez, provides a fuller picture, showing how "Chávez and the farm workers were part of a broad-based, nationally known movement" called La Causa. Griswold del Castillo wrote this section of the book that he and Richard Garcia coauthored.

The pains taken by César were never part of an act. They were a very real extension of his philosophy that human beings are subjects to be taken seriously. —Rev. James Drake

In the summer of 1965, the United States was poised on the brink of a new era. Within a few years the youthful idealism that John Kennedy's brief presidency had inspired changed to a profound disillusionment with the U.S. government. It seemed that Kennedy's New Frontier could not be conquered so easily. For almost a decade, black and white civil rights advocates had been staging sit-ins, boycotts, and marches to protest second-class citizenship. Their hopes had been raised by renewed federal government commitments, and a new Civil Rights Act was due to be signed into law by the president. In Selma, Alabama, Dr. Martin Luther King led a march of 25,000 to the state capitol to protest that state's refusal to follow federal laws. In that protest, two people were killed, adding to the growing number of civil rights martyrs.

Nineteen sixty-five: it was also the year when President Johnson was working on bringing into being his vision of a Great Society, beginning with an assault on poverty. The government created the

Richard Griswold del Castillo, "The Birth of La Causa," in Richard Griswold del Castillo and Richard A. Garcia, *César Chávez: A Triumph of Spirit* (Norman: University of Oklahoma Press, 1995), 41–58.

OEO (Office of Economic Opportunity) that summer, and Congress appropriated $1.3 billion for new educational programs such as Project Head Start and Upward Bound, aimed at raising the educational levels of the poor. The federal government began to pump new money into job-training programs to help the underclass. But this promise proved to be short-lived: President Johnson's growing commitment to Vietnam undercut his domestic reforms. Under the 1964 Gulf of Tonkin Resolution, Congress had given the president authority to "take all necessary measures to repel any armed attack against the forces of the United States." By June 1965, Johnson had sent more than 200,000 United States troops to Vietnam. Some Americans were opposed to the growing involvement and during the summer a coalition of students was working at organizing an antiwar march on Washington. In November, 35,000 people assembled on the mall in front of the Congress to listen to criticism of the president's policies.

This historical moment insured that César Chávez and the farm workers would become part of something called The Movement, a catchall phrase that described those individuals who shared a commitment to end the injustices of racism, the war in Vietnam, the sufferings of the poor, and the degradations of farm workers. During the 1960s Chávez and the NFWU [National Farm Workers Union] — as the FWA [Farm Workers Association] later came to be known — would become one of many lightning rods for a spirit of protest that swept the land. For millions of emerging Mexican-Americans, Chávez became one of the best-known Chicano leaders, a larger-than-life symbol for struggle against exploitation and domination.

Origins of the Delano Grape Strike

The grape strike in Delano grew out of a protest by Filipino workers over wage inequities. Early in 1965, California growers in the Coachella Valley received a temporary dispensation from the Labor Department and had been allowed to import Mexican contract workers — braceros — to harvest the grape crop and to pay them $1.40 an hour. Meanwhile, for the same work, Filipino workers received $1.25 an hour, and Mexican Americans, $1.10. In May, fighting this wage discrimination, AWOC [Agricultural Workers Organizing Committee] went on strike in the Thermal area and after ten days won a raise for both Mexican-American and Filipino workers.

Later in the summer, the grape harvest moved north into the San Joaquin Valley and growers continued to pay the old rate for nonbracero workers. On 8 September, in Delano, AWOC members led by Larry Itliong began a strike against local growers, demanding wage parity. Police began to harass the strikers and growers evicted Filipinos from their labor camps. The Filipinos appealed to Chávez and the Farm Workers Association for support and promised to respect their picket lines. Chávez issued a press release telling members not to work at the struck ranches. *El Malcriado,* the FWA newspaper, published a Spanish translation of Jack London's famous "Definition of a Strikebreaker" to shame potential scabs into not crossing the picket line. Chávez met with his staff to decide whether they should have a general meeting to vote to join the strike. They voted to have the meeting on 16 September, Mexican Independence Day.

For the next few days Chávez traveled constantly, spreading the word about the strike meeting. He prevailed on local Spanish-language disk jockeys to make announcements on their early morning shows: farm workers, irrespective of union membership, were invited to attend the strike meeting. Before the meeting, several FWA work crews had already gone on strike, leaving their jobs before a formal vote.

The evening meeting took place in Delano's Our Lady of Guadalupe church hall—a gathering of more than five hundred farm workers and their families. In an emotional revivalist atmosphere, chants of "Viva La Causa!" echoed before and after speeches in support of the strike. The hall was filled with people of all nationalities and races, blacks, Puerto Ricans, Filipinos, Arabs, and Anglos; but Mexicans and Mexican Americans predominated. Eugene Nelson, a young union volunteer, recorded Chávez's speech at this meeting and later published it in *Huelga:*

> You are here to discuss a matter which is of extreme importance to yourselves, your families and all the community. . . . A hundred and fifty-five years ago, in the state of Guanajuato in Mexico, a padre proclaimed the struggle for liberty. He was killed, but ten years later Mexico won its independence. . . . We Mexicans here in the United States, as well as all other farm laborers, are engaged in another struggle for the freedom and dignity which poverty denies us. But it must not be a violent struggle, even if violence is used against us. . . . The strike was begun by the Filipinos, but it is not exclusively for them. Tonight we must decide if we are to join our fellow workers in this great labor struggle.

Other farm workers rose to speak and added their stories of misery and suffering to the call to join the strike. Representatives of various states in Mexico rose to pledge their support. Chávez explained the sacrifices they would have to make during a strike: the union did not have a strike fund and it would be a long struggle. Nelson recorded what happened next:

"Strike, strike!" the crowd is yelling now. "Huelga, huelga, huelga!"
"All right, we'll take a strike vote then. Everyone who is in favor of going out on strike, raise your right hand...."
If there is a hand not raised, we do not see it.
"Opposed?" The question seems rather foolish by now.
"Que viva la huelga! Long live the strike!" And, "Viva!" the whole auditorium erupts in chorus, the place seems about to tumble down upon our heads.
The cheers continue for a good ten minutes, as pandemonium breaks out: "Viva Mexico! Viva Puerto Rico! Viva la causa! Viva César Chávez! Viva la union!"
The die is cast.

The Strike

Soon after the strike vote, César met with Al Green, the head of AWOC, to coordinate strategy. There were rumors of an impending merger of the two unions, but this was not to take place until the next year. As a result of their discussions, a joint committee to coordinate activities was set up, and the Agricultural Workers Organizing Committee, the AFL-CIO farm workers' union, made its resources available to NFWU members. (The association, as noted in passing above, changed its name to National Farm Workers Union. This event took place in 1966.)

The Delano grape strike covered a 400-square-mile area and involved thousands of workers. The tremendous job of organizing picket lines to patrol the fields fell to inexperienced farm workers and urban volunteers, working side by side. The sheer dimensions of the ranches and farms made it impossible constantly to maintain pickets at all the entrances. Inevitably, scabs *(esquiroles)* found their way into the fields, and the union had to find ways of convincing them to join the strike. The picketed area then became a noisy place. The picketers cajoled, argued, pleaded, orated, and shamed the fieldworkers in Spanish, Tagalog,* and English, trying to get them to join the strike. Picketers walked the dusty borders of the fields holding hand-painted signs, HUELGA, DELANO GRAPE STRIKER, VICTORIA!, accompanied by the FWA black eagle. Always they were observed by the police, who were ready

Tagalog: a language spoken in the Philippines

to arrest picketers entering ranch property. Usually the ranch foreman and his staff would harass the strikers, reviling them with foul language, trying to provoke them into crossing onto farm property. Later the growers hired goons, recruited from the cities, to intimidate the strikers. Violence was a constant possibility and frequent occurrence. Ranch foremen raced their pickup trucks up and down the lines at top speed. They drove tractors between the pickets and the fields to choke the union people with dust. They sprayed them with chemicals and tried to intimidate them with shotguns and dogs. Sometimes they injured strikers. But when someone got hurt on the picket line, it often had the effect of provoking a sympathy walk-out by their own workers. The police almost never intervened to protect the picketers. They photographed the strikers and noted license-plate numbers of the picketers' cars. They arrested picketers for disturbing the peace when they shouted "Huelga!" or read Jack London's strikebreaker definition. The police were clearly in support of the growers.

Chávez saw the picket line as an educational and recruiting experience. It was the place where a person could feel the confrontation between the workers and the growers. It became a way of building a strong membership. He would later say, "The picket line is where a man makes his commitment, and it is irrevocable; the longer he's on the picket line, the stronger the commitment. . . . The picket line is a beautiful thing, because it does something to a human being."

Nonviolence

From the beginning of the strike, Chávez emphasized the importance of nonviolence as a strategy. He exhorted the volunteers and picketers: "If someone commits violence against us, it is much better—if we can—not to react against the violence but to react in such a way as to get closer to our goal. People don't like to see a nonviolent movement subjected to violence, and there's a lot of support across the country for nonviolence. That's the key point we have going for us. We can turn the world if we can do it nonviolently."

Chávez's faith in nonviolence came from his mother's influence, his religious faith, and his self-education in reading Gandhi and other pacifists. In 1965, nonviolence also was a practical tactic for rallying national support for a labor strike. Nonviolence had become an important characteristic of the civil rights movement and it was fast becoming a tactic of the antiwar movement, although in both movements nonviolent protests would increasingly escalate into violent confrontations. For Chávez, nonviolence meant time-consuming organization and training. He used Gandhi's phrase *moral jujitsu* to describe its effect on the opposition: "Always hit the opposition off balance, but keep your principles." Chávez's commitment to nonviolence became stronger and deeper as the years passed—became more a personal article of faith, more spiritual, almost an end in itself. He told a union meeting in 1969, "There is no such thing as means and ends. Everything that we do is an end, in itself, that we can never erase. That is why we must make all our actions the kind we would like to be judged on, although they might be our last—which they might well be, who knows? That is why we will not let ourselves be provoked by our adversaries into behaving hatefully."

Volunteers

During the early days of the strike, hundreds of volunteers descended on Delano to participate. Many were clergy, responding to the message of the new liberation theology. Churchmen from the migrant ministry arrived, reporting that there was growing church support for the strike. Priests from barrio parishes traveled to the fields to offer help from the inner city. Fr. Victor Salandini volunteered to be a lobbyist in Washington, D.C. Other volunteers offered their services as legal consultants and in public relations. The Student Nonviolent Coordinating Committee (SNCC) and the Congress of Racial Equality sent messages of support. Later they sent volunteers. César argued with his staff about the value of the volunteers. He wanted a diversity of energies and ideas. "If we were nothing but farm workers in the Union now, just Mexican farm workers, we'd have about 30 percent of all the ideas we have. There would be no cross-fertilization, no growing. It's beautiful to work with other groups, other ideas and other customs. It's like the wood is laminated."

One of the early student volunteers to join the strike was a young Chicano from the San Francisco Bay Area named Luis Valdez. Originally from Delano, he had grown up in a migrant family but had escaped from the fields to the city and become a university student and member of the radical theater group, the San Francisco Mime Troupe. He took a creative energy to Delano that soon resulted in the organization of El Teatro Campesino (The Farm Workers Theater). Valdez had the idea of using simple, one-act skits, or *actos*, to educate farm workers about the union and the issues involved in the strike. The teatro, performed on the back of a flatbed truck in the fields, was an effective way of reaching farm workers. The actos were improvisa-tions that dramatized, often in uproariously funny and ironic ways, the lives and struggles of field workers. The actors were them-selves campesinos (farm workers): Felipe Cantu, Agustín Lira, Errol Franklin, and Gilbert Rubio were actor-founders. The teatro members followed the harvest to help with recruitment of union members. They toured the larger towns and cities to raise funds for the union, visiting university campuses and the urban barrios. In Delano, Valdez set up a Centro Campesino Cultural (Farm Worker Cultural Center) to teach migrant children about their Mexican heritage through art, music, dance, and *teatro.* He explained the need for this effort: "This is a soci-ety largely hostile to our cultural values. There is no poetry about the United States. No depth, no faith, no allowance for human contrari-ness. No soul, no mariachi, no chili sauce, no pulque,* no mysticism, no *chingaderas* (fooling around)." Luis stayed with the NFWU for sev-eral years and then moved his group to San Juan Bautista. Later he broke into Hollywood with his stage production, *Zoot Suit,* and the movie, *La Bamba.*

The Strike Becomes National

César's main activity during the early months of the strike was to travel around the state to the college campuses to give speeches and galvanize support for the striking workers. In October, he and Wendy Gospel drove from Delano to the Bay Area where he spoke at U.C. Berkeley, San Francisco State, Mills College in Oakland, and Stanford University. They raised more than $6,500 in donations and got stu-dents to flood the Delano chief of police with phone calls and letters protesting the arrest of strikers. Chávez's speaking style had changed very little from his CSO days. He was not an emotional speaker. He convinced students to support the union through his sincerity, humil-ity, and command of the facts about the struggle between the farm workers and the growers. His low-key approach was disarming in an age of radical and flamboyant rhetoric.

The national news media helped in generating support for the strike. Television news crews filmed the drama of the confrontations at the picket line. An NBC special, "The Harvest of Shame," depicted the tragic conditions of migrant laborers in the United States and helped to make people more aware of the farm workers' plight.

pulque: an alcoholic beverage made from the sap of various agaves

Reporters from city newspapers and national magazines interviewed Chávez and other union officials as well as the growers. Chávez spoke about how the farm workers were fighting for their civil rights and economic justice. The farm worker movement dovetailed with the growing national concern about civil rights.

Publicity became increasingly important when the union launched a boycott to put pressure on the growers to recognize the union and sign contracts. They targeted the most identifiable grape products from the largest Delano growers, the Schenley Corporation, the Di Giorgio Corporation, S & W Fine Foods, and TreeSweet. The success of the boycott depended on an informed and sympathetic consumer.

Early in the strike, national union leader Walter Reuther, head of the United Auto Workers, visited Delano (December 1965) and this brought national attention to the strike and boycott. Reuther was on the West Coast to attend the AFL-CIO midwinter convention in San Francisco and he had heard about the strike in Delano of Filipino and Mexican workers. For Reuther, the farm-labor movement reminded him of the labor militancy that the United Auto Workers had undertaken during the 1930s. With the urging of Paul Schrade, the UAW representative in California, he convinced the UAW to donate money to the strike. He traveled to Delano to present the check to Chávez and Al Green, the AWOC director. FWA and AWOC members met him at the airport and, in violation of the orders of the local police chief, prepared to stage a march through Delano to the union headquarters. Reuther held an FWA sign and marched next to Chávez and hundreds of supporters, surrounded by newspaper and television reporters who expected a confrontation. When they met the chief of police, the chief decided to back down. At the city hall, in front of the mayor and other dignitaries, Reuther gave a dramatic speech supporting the strike demands. Later, at Filipino Hall he held a press conference and, at César's request, agreed to meet with the growers to get them to settle the strike. Chávez later rated Reuther's support that day as the event that gave the grape strike its first wide national visibility.

The March on Sacramento

Other dramatic events gave momentum to the strike and boycott. Three months after Reuther's visit, on 16 March 1966, Chávez organized a march from Delano to Sacramento to dramatize the strike and get the support of California Governor Pat Brown. The march was a tactic Chávez had used with the CSO during the Oxnard struggle.

Besides its practical political value, the march was linked to the idea of sacrifice. In Chávez's words, "This was an excellent way of training ourselves to endure the long, long struggle. . . . This was a penance more than anything else—and it was quite a penance, because there was an awful lot of suffering involved in this pilgrimage, a great deal of pain." In the spirit of the Lenten season, the march became a religious pilgrimage. It was planned to end on Easter Sunday, covering 250 miles in twenty-five days.

Chávez marched with the procession as it left Delano. Filipino, Mexican, African American, and Anglo members marched enthusiastically. They carried the U.S. and Mexican flags, the FWA and AWOC banners, and a flag with the image of the Virgin of Guadalupe. The march helped recruit more members and it spread the spirit of the strike. As they passed through the farming country of the San Joaquin Valley, at each small town hundreds of workers greeted them. Some joined the march and carried the flags to the next town. At night they had rallies with music, singing, speeches, and a dramatic reading of "El Plan de Delano" that Luis Valdez had composed in the spirit of Emiliano Zapata's "Plan de Ayala," a declaration of the agrarian revolution in 1910. The march generated spirit. The occupants of passing cars, if they supported the boycott and strike, would wave and honk; supporters of the growers would curse and make obscene gestures. By and large, there was local support, with hundreds of touching incidents. In one town a man and his daughters gave the marchers a drink of punch from a crystal bowl with cups. People working in the fields as the marchers passed by gave up their jobs and joined the procession.

For César, the Sacramento march was a painful ordeal. After the first couple of days his old shoes gave him blisters and one of his feet swelled considerably. Since he considered it a penitential walk, he refused to take medication to lessen the pain. By the end of the third day his leg was swollen and his blisters began to bleed. He was running a temperature. By the seventh day his physical condition was such that a nurse ordered him to ride in a station wagon for the rest of the march. He briefly rested in the station wagon, bitterly disappointed with himself. The next day he rejoined the marchers.

By the time the marchers reached Stockton, a few days from their goal, there were more than five thousand of them, singing, chanting, and waving as they walked. Chávez remembered: "People were getting in front of us with flowers. There were mariachis playing. It was a fiesta." That night in Stockton, Chávez got a phone call from Sidney Korshak, a representative of the Schenley Corporation. Korshak said,

"I want to talk to you about recognizing the union and signing a contract." César thought it was a joke and hung up. But Korshak called back and they arranged a meeting in Beverly Hills the next day. After driving during the night to get there, César found himself in Korshak's home with Bill Kircher, the AFL-CIO's representative, and a Teamster representative. The Teamsters Union had helped the strikers by refusing to work Schenley's warehouse in San Francisco. Korshak said that Schenley was ready to sign a contract; the question was, with which union? Kircher tried to pressure Chávez into letting AWOC get the contract, but César convinced Kircher to compromise and let Schenley recognize the FWA and let AWOC be a signatory as a witness: that way, Kircher could save face with his union. On 7 April the agreement was made public. In a triumphant mood, the pilgrimage ended a few days later on the steps of the state capitol. They had won their first victory and demonstrated the power of their cause. Governor Brown avoided meeting the marchers by going to Palm Springs to spend the weekend with Frank Sinatra: they held their celebration without him.

Schenley had been pressured into a contract by the FWA boycott. In particular, a rumor had been started that bartenders in New York were going to refuse to serve Schenley products in sympathy with the strike and this threat convinced the company to give in. For the first time in U.S. history, a grassroots, farm-labor union had gained recognition by a corporation (some years before, in Hawaii, the Longshoremen's Union had gotten a contract for pineapple workers).

Di Giorgio, the Teamsters, and a Merger

Three days after the conclusion of the march, Chávez turned his attention to the largest grower in the Delano area, the Di Giorgio Corporation. Di Giorgio was a family-controlled company that had extensive holdings throughout California and Florida. The most important grape ranches that would become targets of the grape strike were located in Sierra Vista, Arvin, near Delano, and one ranch near Borrego Springs. The Di Giorgios also had thousands of acres of pears, plums, apricots, and citrus trees. They marketed their products under the S & W Fine Foods and TreeSweet labels. In 1965, the Di Giorgio Corporation netted $231 million. Robert Di Giorgio, the patriarch of the family, was on the board of directors of the Bank of America. The Di Giorgio family had successfully broken strikes and unions since the 1930s and Steinbeck, in his novel, *The Grapes of Wrath,* had used Di Giorgio as a model for the grower Gregorio.

Chávez was convinced of the power of the boycott and soon hundreds of volunteers who remembered previous struggles against the Di Giorgios joined the boycott drive. Within a short time the company agreed to enter into negotiations to have a union election, but Chávez broke off talks when company guards attacked a picketer at Sierra Vista. When negotiations resumed, Chávez discovered that Di Giorgio had invited the Teamsters to recruit members in the vineyards. He ended the negotiations in protest.

In California, New York, and the Midwest, Teamster locals had been supportive of the NFWA during the early months of the grape strike, but now the national Teamsters organization decided to organize farm workers to protect their members working as packers and as truckers. Almost one-fifth of all Teamster members worked in industries that were dependent on agriculture. The independent NFWA, with its strikes and boycotts, was a threat to the nonfield workers whose jobs depended on the harvest. In the parlance of labor organizers, the Teamsters entered the fields to "protect their flanks."

The Teamsters had helped break strikes before. In 1961 they had signed a "sweetheart" contract with Bud Antle, the largest grower of lettuce in California, to break a strike. This pattern seemed to be happening again. Beginning in mid-1966 the two unions, the Teamsters and the NFWA, began a jurisdictional fight that, on and off, lasted more than ten years, resulting in violence, injury, and several deaths.

Di Giorgio's strategy was to rush quickly into an election to determine union representation, having the assurance that the Teamsters would win. The Teamsters, in turn, would give him a contract which benefited the company. When Chávez learned of this move he rallied the union to boycott the elections, scheduled for 24 June: those who were on strike were not to be eligible to vote and essentially, only those who had already signed Teamster authorization cards would cast a ballot in favor of a union contract. The ensuing NFWA–AWOC boycott turned away almost half of the eligible voters and the union began lobbying the state governor to investigate the election and have it overturned. It was an election year, 1966, and Governor Brown was running against Ronald Reagan. He needed all the support he could get. Under pressure from the Mexican-American Political Association, lobbied by Dolores Huerta, Pat Brown agreed to launch an investigation, with the result, two weeks later, of a recommendation that the elections be invalidated and that a new election date be set for 30 August. Under the new agreement, any worker who had worked for Di Giorgio for fifteen days before the strike was eligible to vote, meaning that almost two thousand strikers would be able to cast their ballots.

Prior to the election, in 1966, to consolidate power AWOC and the NFWU formally merged to form a united union within the AFL-CIO. This move was not without controversy and danger. César was worried that within the AFL-CIO the union would be subject to regulations that would prohibit the boycott. Some of the student volunteers, especially the liberals and radicals, were very much opposed to merging their movement with organized labor. César's staff split on the issue. Marshall Ganz, a Harvard-educated civil rights worker in charge of the international boycott, was in favor of the merger. Jim Drake, Chávez's adviser, was against it. The migrant ministry staff supported it. César realized that the rank and file had to be educated to the benefits of the merger before they would agree. With about a month left before the 30 August election, César decided to ask for a vote and not a single farm worker voted against the reorganization.

Under the merger agreement, a new organization, called the United Farm Workers Organizing Committee (UFWOC—eventually to become the United Farm Workers of America, AFL-CIO) was formed, with Chávez as the director. The new organization continued with strategies of the older NFWA. When the AWOC staff learned that their salaries were going to be reduced and that they would have to give up their plush expense accounts, they resigned (an exception was Larry Itliong). Chávez explained his philosophy of leadership to the new staff: "The job can't be done unless there is a commitment. If we're going to lead people and ask them to starve and really sacrifice, we've got to do it first, do it more than anybody else, because it isn't the orders, it isn't the pronouncements, it's the deeds that count."

With the merger, the new UFWOC became truly a multiethnic union. Most of the AWOC members were Filipino, and most of the NFWA were Mexican. César had to argue against those who wanted to keep the union controlled by Mexicans. César told them that the Filipinos had to be represented in all the union activities and services. Most of the Mexicans went along with the integration of leadership and services, but a few were ready to quit the union in protest. From the beginning, César had not thought of La Causa as a movement that would be motivated primarily by appeals to race or nationality. When César had worked for the CSO, he had confronted the issue of Mexican chauvinism and had been uncompromising in fighting for the inclusion of blacks within the organization. Although the core leadership of the NFWA was Mexican-American, the staff and hundreds of volunteer workers were predominantly Anglo.

The merger strategy paid off with an election victory at Di Giorgio's farms. The UFWOC volunteers had worked arduously to round up former employees of the company and migrant families who had heard of the impending elections traveled from as far as central Mexico to cast their ballots. On election day, the union ran a shuttle service to pick up workers to take them to the polling place. The next day, supervised by the arbitration association, they counted the ballots in San Francisco: UFWOC had won, getting 530 votes to the Teamsters' 331. Only 12 workers voted to not have a union. That day there was a huge celebration in Filipino Hall in Delano, but there still remained the problem of negotiating a satisfactory contract with Di Giorgio. The boycott would continue for another four years, when a contract was signed. At least for now, victory was sweet.

Shortly after the victory, César received a congratulatory telegram from Dr. Martin Luther King Jr. In part King said, "You and your valiant fellow workers have demonstrated your commitment to righting grievous wrongs forced upon exploited people. We are together with you in spirit and in determination that our dreams for a better tomorrow will be realized."

But in August 1966, the "dreams of a better tomorrow" were beginning to look like nightmares. The civil rights movement, so full of promise a year earlier, was taking a violent turn. That summer, bloody race riots erupted in major U.S. cities. The philosophy of nonviolence was being denounced by new black militants: Stokely Carmichael and H. Rap Brown in the Student Nonviolent Coordinating Committee; and Bobby Seale and Huey Newton of the Black Panther movement. Malcolm X, too, leader of the Black Muslims who was assassinated in 1965, also had not looked kindly on nonviolence. On campuses, the opposition to the war in Vietnam and racism became more vocal. Students organized peace marches and teach-ins, burned draft cards, and demonstrated against ROTC and military recruiters.

Meanwhile, a nationwide Chicano movement was beginning to take shape with La Causa at the forefront. In New Mexico, a fiery Baptist preacher, Reies López Tijerina, had organized Hispanos to regain the lands they had lost after the American takeover in 1848. The Alianza Federal de Mercedes Libres, established in 1963, claimed more than twenty thousand members. Under Tijerina's leadership the alliance began to be more militant in its tactics. In July 1966 they had organized a march of sixty-two miles from Albuquerque to Santa Fe to demand that the state government investigate the theft of land grants. Within a few months, Tijerina and his followers occupied federal lands and declared an independent Hispano nation, the Republic of San Joaquín del Rio de Chama.

In Colorado, a former middleweight boxing champion, Rodolfo "Corky" Gonzales, in 1966 founded the Denver Crusade for Justice, a civil rights group dedicated to the promotion of Chicano liberation and nationalism. Gonzales appealed to the urban barrios in his attacks on the inadequacies of the school system and police brutality. His epic poem, *I Am Joaquín,* was an inspirational message calling for a reaffirmation of identity and pride. Like Luis Valdez with his Centro Campesino, Gonzales established a cultural center that functioned as an alternative school, La Escuela de Tlatelolco, La Plaza de las Tres Culturas. Unlike Chávez and the UFWOC, Gonzales appealed to Chicano ethnic consciousness to form a Chicano nation.

Thus, by the end of 1966 Chávez and the farm workers were part of a broad-based, nationally known movement. La Causa of the farm workers became part of the agenda for scores of local Chicano movement organizations. The UFW black eagle appeared at almost every Chicano rally and would become an icon of the Chicano movement. Chávez's leadership had galvanized widespread support beyond the Mexican-American communities, including student radicals, liberals, clerics, and organized labor. Together they had produced some limited victories, but the conflict was far from over. In some respects, it was just beginning.

MARGARET ROSE

César Chávez and Dolores Huerta: Partners in "La Causa"

2001

No one worked more closely with Chávez than Dolores Huerta. A dynamic, nontraditional Chicana, Huerta was an outstanding, tough-minded negotiator. As Margaret Rose, the leading authority on women's roles in the farmworkers' movement makes clear, Huerta and Chávez gradually realized that they could work closely on projects to organize Mexican American workers. Later, Huerta's blunt, no-nonsense approach to field labor problems shaped her views of Chávez. Although they vigorously differed, and sometimes vociferously argued, over which techniques

Margaret Rose, a staff member at the University of California, Santa Barbara, wrote this essay specifically for this book.

to use and which goals to attain, Huerta and Chávez respected each other. Huerta, Rose concludes, obviously endorsed Chávez's "core values, beliefs, and philosophy." Like most of those who worked closely with Chávez, Huerta marveled at his "commitment, cooperation, perseverance, and integrity."

United Farm Workers (UFW) historians have located the origins of the movement to organize California's farmworkers in César Chávez's dramatic resignation from the directorship of the Community Service Organization (CSO) in March 1962 and the launching of the Farm Workers Association (FWA). As Chávez later revealed in an interview, Dolores Huerta contributed significantly to this effort: "Dolores and I were the architects of the National Farm Workers Association."[1] Huerta played a major role not only in designing the organization but also in running it. Although Chávez was chosen general director of the group, Huerta served as vice president and the only female elected official. In the early years of the group's existence, the two consulted frequently on basic decisions: the name, the incorporation of the FWA, its constitution, dues setting, group insurance benefits, credit union, fund-raising, organizing strategies, and political tactics. Repeatedly, Huerta sought advice from her network of contacts in northern California and conveyed legal information and made recommendations to Chávez.

Huerta's close collaboration with Chávez placed her in a unique position to observe and comment on him and his actions. On the way to explaining how she interpreted Chávez, this essay will also reveal her very important role in the emergence of the union. As a strong-willed and independent thinker, she felt intensely about issues of poverty, injustice, and exploitation. An articulate and educated woman, she did not hesitate to offer opinions. During the time the FWA was getting off the ground, Huerta lived and worked in Stockton, California, while Chávez set up its headquarters in Delano. This separation necessitated frequent communication by mail. The existence of the unique and detailed correspondence of more than fifty letters from Huerta to Chávez during the almost three years the two were establishing the FWA provides fascinating glimpses into her view of his leadership, the personal sacrifices they made, the tenuous nature of

---

[1]Jacques E. Levy, *Cesar Chavez: Autobiography of La Causa* (New York: W. W. Norton, 1975), 166.

their early efforts, their disagreements, and their complex working relationship.[2] Perhaps misguided by early treatments of the farm-workers movement that focused largely on Chávez, historians have missed the importance of this partnership. Scholars now have the opportunity to evaluate more accurately the relationship between these two social activists. These documents reveal how Chávez, and by extension the farmworkers, benefited from a dedicated confidante and an outspoken Chicana advocate.

Huerta's esteem for Chávez derived from her respect for his leader-ship of the CSO, the self-help association that emerged in Mexican American barrios in the post–World War II era throughout the South-west. The CSO sparked Chávez's and Huerta's social consciences and provided an avenue to civic activism. Starting as a volunteer in San Jose, Chávez became an organizer and later general director of the group.[3] Huerta's entry into community involvement centered in Stockton, where she volunteered in voter registration drives, educa-tional campaigns, and chapter fund-raising. Her abilities and passion for social justice attracted attention, so she was offered the position of lobbyist.[4]

Huerta's first reaction to Chávez was not promising. "I found César was very shy," she noted to a journalist. "The first two or three years I knew him it was difficult to have a conversation with him."[5] Increas-ingly, their paths crossed at numerous meetings, conventions, and campaigns. During this time, Huerta's interests broadened when sev-eral of her Stockton CSO colleagues and other socially conscious citi-zens formed the Agricultural Workers Association (AWA) in 1958. This local interest group dissolved when the AFL-CIO–sponsored Agricultural Workers Organizing Committee (AWOC) emerged a year later. Former AWA members enlisted in the campaign, including Huerta, who became secretary-treasurer. She soon grew disenchanted with the leadership, direction, and policies, however, and resigned

[2]This set of correspondence is part of the National Farm Workers Association papers, housed at the Archives of Labor and Urban Affairs, Walter P. Reuther Library, Detroit, Box 2, Correspondence Huerta to Chávez, 1962–1964 (hereafter cited as ALUA). Most of these letters are undated. Unless otherwise noted, the quoted material in this essay comes from this source.

[3]Peter Matthiessen, *Sal Si Puedes: Cesar Chavez and the New American Revolution* (New York: Random House, 1969), 45–49.

[4]Margaret Eleanor Rose, "Women in the United Farm Workers: A Study of Chicana and Mexicana Participation in a Labor Union, 1950 to 1980" (Ph.D. diss., University of California, Los Angeles, 1988), 34–39.

[5]Ronald B. Taylor, *Chavez and the Farm Workers* (Boston: Beacon Press, 1975), 88.

from the group.[6] As Huerta worked more closely with Chávez, a common bond developed. Their experiences, their unswerving commitment to the Mexican American community, a shared outrage for the abject conditions of farmworkers, and their impatience with the ineffectual policies of the past further united them. Frustrated by the failure of the CSO to support an internal initiative to organize farmworkers and by the misguided approaches of the AWOC, they turned their energies to the campesinos (farm laborers).

Swept up in the idealism and reform then associated with Lyndon Johnson's Great Society programs and civil rights movements, Chávez and Huerta embarked on a journey that would test their resolve and stress their families' financial and emotional lives. Exhibiting her characteristic optimism, Huerta enthusiastically embraced this challenge to unionize California's agricultural laborers. In Chávez, she had found a colleague willing to dedicate himself body and soul to a cause—a trait she identified in herself. Pleased and humbled, she wrote to him, "It looks like working for the Association is just the job I need. Whether my assistance will be of value, is another question."

Establishing the financial viability of the FWA proved to be a far more difficult task than either could have imagined. Eschewing outside assistance, Chávez and Huerta believed that the fledgling organization had to stand on its own. She admired his quiet strength, single-mindedness, and determination. Clearly, the personal costs of this decision were high. After depleting their unemployment insurance and savings, Chávez and his wife, Helen, along with their eight children, faced financial difficulties. "Helen," Chávez wrote his CSO mentor Fred Ross in August 1962, "is now working a few hours every day out in the fields. She is cutting grapes and works from about 6:00 in the morning till about 1 in the afternoon."[7] In the afternoons, Helen sought employment assembling cardboard boxes in a packing shed. When the grape season ended, she engaged in other piecework jobs. After school and during the summers, her older children joined her in the harvests. And at times when finances were particularly desperate, Chávez took time off from running the Delano office to work in the fields. Family illness further strained the household income. Learning of Helen's illness, Huerta recommended hiring her after her recovery to assist with the FWA bookkeeping. "It would be a good way to get

---

[6]Dick Meister and Anne Loftis, *A Long Time Coming: The Struggle to Unionize America's Farm Workers* (New York: Macmillan, 1977), 92–96.

[7]César Chávez to Fred Ross, 17 August 1962, Box 3, Series I, Folder 6, Fred Ross Collection, ALUA.

the work done," she thought, "and also help out your family." Given the limited FWA revenue, even these strategies were not sufficient to keep the family solvent. Both César's and Helen's families contributed groceries, clothes, and child care to supplement their insufficient income.[8]

Huerta shared in their reduced circumstances. Recognizing their bleak prospects, Chávez persuaded her to stay on the CSO payroll until the financial outlook of the FWA improved.[9] The Chávez family was not alone in their marginal existence. Huerta, in her thirties, with seven children and an estranged second husband (whom she later divorced), also shouldered considerable financial burdens. She harbored grave reservations about Chávez's plans for her continued employment with the CSO. Fred Ross endorsed the idea, but only if Huerta fulfilled her current duties for the Stockton chapter. This, in effect, meant that she had to work two jobs while receiving the salary of one. She reluctantly agreed to the arrangement but expressed misgivings. "Everyone seems to think I can take care of the [CSO] office and the farm worker project . . . and I'm not sure I can," she said frankly to Chávez. Her reservations centered not only on the "killer schedule" and the greater lack of control over her activities, but also on the conflict of interest created by her continuing relationship with an organization Chávez had left because of its failure to organize farmworkers. "I feel there will be a lot of criticism," she continued. "If I did not have to work for the CSO, but could have an independent income, then no one could say anything about what I do." Coaxed by Chávez, she endured as long as she could. But her initial apprehensions eventually proved justified. "I am to be terminated," she noted tersely to Chávez.

Huerta's correspondence with Chávez reveals a constant struggle to make ends meet. Her finances took a turn for the worse when her unemployment check from the CSO job ran out. She proposed a solution. "What I wanted to ask you," she wrote to Chávez, "was if I could charge $5.00 for some of the cases [dealing with members' immigration and welfare problems]. Not for everyone, but if I could get $15.00 per week . . . that would be enough. However, I believe it is much more important to get members plus loyalty, so don't feel bad in telling me no. I will manage somehow." Chávez's response was no. He believed that working on such problems made people dependent—a

[8]Margaret Rose, "Traditional and Nontraditional Patterns of Female Activism in the United Farm Workers of America, 1962 to 1980," *Frontiers* 11 (No. 1, 1990): 27–28.
[9]Taylor, *Chavez and the Farm Workers,* 105.

view that contrasted with Huerta's more service-oriented approach—
and detracted from organizing efforts. Support, however irregular,
came from her two former husbands, family members, and friends.
She augmented these sources with temporary translation assignments, substitute teaching, and even a brief stint in the onion harvest,
in addition to her work for the FWA.

While Chávez concentrated on workers in the Delano area, Huerta
organized workers from her base in Stockton. Her letters describe the
long days and nights publicizing the new organization, setting up
meetings, calling on workers in their homes, and visiting labor camps
in farmworker towns such as Acampo, Woodbridge, Manteca, Victor,
Linden, and Lodi, in addition to covering Stockton. Her correspondence also describes the frustrations endured as a result of the lack of
basic needs for a farm labor organizer—reliable transportation and
communication. Huerta and Chávez commiserated on the simple tools
that most took for granted. "Right now I have three handicaps," she
bluntly asserted to Chávez, "no car, no typewriter, no phone." A car in
need of a mechanic and a delinquent phone bill brought her work to a
standstill. Help from her brother and a family friend ended those temporary, but frequent, impediments. In response to similar woes from
Chávez, she immediately sympathized: "Sorry to hear about your car.
Should we try to get some money for repairs?" She offered to take up
a collection and send the money to Delano. Both were always scram-
bling for gas money and overextending the FWA credit card.

Huerta's financial problems continued. Even with a used car she
purchased with a $100 auto loan, building up support for the group
was slow and arduous because of the reluctance of some workers to
get involved and because organizational meetings were often canceled
at the last minute because of a misunderstanding or other unexpected
glitch. "Thursday night's meeting was also a fluke," she lamented in
what was becoming a common complaint. "Only the fellow who would
give the meeting was there, but he is going to try again. (Ain't this a
bitch?)"

Canceled meetings and worker apathy were occupational hazards
for both, but Huerta also had to contend with resistance to a female
organizer. In Stockton, she ignored and outlasted this reluctance, but
the issue arose again whenever she targeted a new area. A house
meeting in Modesto, attended primarily by men, abruptly terminated
when she appeared at the scheduled hour. The participants did not try
to conceal their motives, stating openly their refusal to meet with a

woman.[10] As in Stockton, she did not allow such hostility to deter her and doggedly persisted in her efforts. Although women's issues were emerging in this decade, gender consciousness was not yet as widespread as it would later become. Revealingly, Chávez did not consider this type of discrimination as a distinct obstacle for women. Huerta herself only gradually came to recognize this additional barrier female organizers confronted.

A functioning car, gas money, a working telephone, and a typewriter—mundane items, yet they were central to the operation of the FWA. These tools helped generate the dues that were critical to the survival of the effort. Huerta included dues in almost every letter she sent to Delano during these years. "I hope this letter finds you in the best of health," she wrote, "and not close to a nervous breakdown over the coming dues collections." As she well knew, the $3.50 monthly expense was not easy for workers to pledge because of their meager wages, their fear of employers' retaliation, competition from other unions, the unpredictable nature of agricultural employment, labor surpluses, and unexpected illnesses and family emergencies. As a result, union members frequently missed payments. They also moved around the state in search of work, leading to additional bookkeeping problems. Despite the disappointing, irregular, and inadequate collections, after deducting expenses, Chávez and Huerta shared the slim proceeds. Commenting in an interview, Huerta adamantly stated, "César was very fair about that. He would always divide it down the middle."[11]

Although Huerta shared with Chávez a deep commitment to unionizing field laborers, she differed with him on politics. When not organizing workers, Huerta lobbied political officials, an atypical avocation for a Mexican American woman at the time, but one at which she became unusually adept. "Everyone knows her," observed Chávez following a trip to the state capital in December 1962, "and the usual remark is that she is a fighter."[12] He remained more ambivalent regarding the political arena as an effective avenue for achieving significant change.

Despite Chávez's reservations, Huerta maintained an avid interest in the political process. She had first gained exposure to lobbying as

---

[10]Dolores Huerta, interview by author, Keene, Calif., 8 Feb. 1985.
[11]Taylor, *Chavez and the Farm Workers,* 101.
[12]Chávez to Ross, 14 Dec. 1962, Box 3, Series I, Folder 10, Ross Collection, ALUA.

a legislative advocate for the CSO in the late 1950s. By the time of her association with the FWA, her skills had become almost legendary. Huerta took pride in her successful invasion of the male world of Sacramento politics, and she proved to be successful in her struggles on behalf of old-age pensions, a higher minimum wage for field workers, and aid to dependent children of unemployed agricultural workers.

Even though Chávez recognized Huerta's political talents, he did not encourage her lobbying efforts because they took time away from field organizing and perhaps also because he resented the public attention she received. To Huerta, the state capitol was a place where she was not only effective but also removed from the male workers whom she tried to organize and who resisted an independent female labor leader. The elected officials, by contrast, listened to and frequently voted for legislation she supported. Their greater openness offered her an opportunity to exercise more professional and political autonomy away from unreceptive farm laborers and from Chávez himself.

Huerta carried her lobbying efforts beyond California to the nation's capital. When Johnson's Great Society programs gained momentum in the 1960s, federal agencies tapped her expertise on the conditions of Mexican Americans in general and farmworkers in particular. She took advantage of her entrée to advance the interests of Mexican, Mexican American, and FWA workers testifying before committees and meeting with individual lawmakers. Among the issues of greatest concern was Public Law 78.[13] Enacted by Congress in 1951, the law extended a World War II program to regulate the annual importation of farm laborers from Mexico. In the late 1950s and early 1960s, opposition mounted against the legislation from labor, civic, ethnic, and religious groups, as well as from the leadership within the Democratic party. Huerta was among those attacking the program at the state and national levels. Congress eventually ended it in 1965.[14] Overall, Huerta's enthusiasm for legislative action caused friction with Chávez. "We probably should have made the decision," she contended, "that my work in the field was more important [than] the legislative work before I started." She remained more confident and more comfortable engaging the political system than he did.

[13]See Ernesto Galarza, *Merchants of Labor* (Charlotte, Calif.: McNally and Loftin, 1964).
[14]Linda C. Majka and Theo J. Majka, *Farm Workers, Agribusiness, and the State* (Philadelphia: Temple University Press, 1982), 151–66.

Operating on a shoestring, making decisions on a trial and error basis, creating a union from the ground up, and adapting tactics from the civil rights movement, Chávez and Huerta were both dedicated and strong-willed individuals. Though exhibiting mutual respect, collaborating as closely as they did under difficult circumstances, they were bound to have misunderstandings, conflicting points of view, and arguments. But for the organization to survive, it was crucial to negotiate their differences.

Although Huerta may have felt deference toward Chávez initially, as the struggle to unionize farmworkers advanced, she did not hesitate to speak her mind. Many supporters within and outside the organization increasingly held Chávez in awe, but Huerta characteristically confronted him and questioned his ideas and decisions. "To further finish up my peeves," she wrote after a miscommunication during an FWA board meeting in Delano, "I also resent it when you are not honest with me. . . . I do not mind playing the part of the heavy if I know why and when I am supposed to take on this role." To her credit, Huerta did not bear grudges and could move forward after venting her grievances. Having a trusted and forthright colleague who was willing to work behind the scenes to negotiate sensitive internal and personnel matters gave Chávez more room to maneuver. Huerta's candid assessments also expanded the range of options in developing strategies to combat agribusiness and its political allies.

As a forceful and self-assured person, Huerta could tolerate criticism. "I received your penitent letter, much to my surprise, and as the natives say, 'no hay fijon' [pay it no mind]," she responded to one reproach from Chávez. "I deserve the recriminations. Furthermore, I think I am still ahead when it comes to losing tempers." Although she appreciated Chávez's apology, Huerta preferred to work under pressure and accepted the tensions and strains that inevitably emerged under such circumstances. Obviously, Chávez benefited from her frankness and toughness. Her attitude created a more open environment for airing opinions, exchanging views, and arriving at a decision.

From 1962 to 1964, Huerta proved an integral part of the emergence and development of the FWA. From her Stockton base, she sought legal advice and assistance on the incorporation of the organization, conferred with various representatives to obtain information on group insurance policies, supported favorable legislative initiatives in Sacramento and Washington, D.C., recruited new members, collected dues from established supporters, traveled to Delano for board meetings, and regularly consulted with Chávez on the progress and direction of the group. She did all this while raising a family of seven children, eventually as a single parent. Her family would grow still larger in the 1970s.[15]

Huerta felt comfortable with this working relationship, she valued the cause, and she respected Chávez. Despite the hardships and their disagreements, she believed that she could work with him and make a difference in the lives of impoverished farmworkers. Perhaps this is why she finally succumbed to repeated pressures from Chávez to relocate to the southern San Joaquin Valley.

In 1964, Huerta finally agreed with Chávez's view that the FWA's success required a more concentrated effort in Delano and greater visibility of the organization's message through the dissemination of a newspaper. This decision required Huerta to uproot her family from Stockton and, when Chávez could find no one else suitable for the weekly paper, to add writing to her responsibilities. Huerta assented to the move but only after school was out.[16]

Even then, Huerta found it difficult to resettle her children, to leave her extended family and social network in Stockton, and to begin anew the tasks of locating child care and housing. She lived temporarily in the crowded Chávez household until she could find and afford her own housing.[17] She also regretted having to curtail her political lobbying and relinquish the greater independence that the physical separation from the Delano headquarters had permitted. Yet the shift to the southern San Joaquin Valley offered greater efficiency, direction, and focus for building the FWA.

Chávez and Huerta, with a small core of supporters, now prepared for the time when they could launch a coordinated drive to change the lives of farmworkers—a contest that came far sooner than they had anticipated. The opportunity arose when the rival AFL-CIO–sponsored AWOC, with a predominantly Filipino membership, went on strike and asked for FWA support. The consequent cooperation resulted in the famous Delano grape strike of 1965, the subsequent creation of the United Farm Workers Organizing Committee (UFWOC), and the beginning of a new era in César Chávez's life, as well as in Dolores Huerta's.[18]

---

[15]Margaret Rose, "Dolores Huerta," in *Notable Hispanic American Women,* ed. Diane Telgen and Jim Kamp (Detroit: Gale Research, 1993), 212. Huerta would eventually bear four more children when she began a relationship with Richard Chávez in the 1970s.

[16]Joan London and Henry Anderson, *So Shall Ye Reap* (New York: Thomas Y. Crowell, 1970), 149.

[17]Dolores Huerta, interview by author, Keene, Calif., 4 Feb. 1985.

[18]See Eugene Nelson, *Huelga: The First Hundred Days of the Great Delano Strike* (Delano, Calif.: Farm Worker Press, 1966).

At the outset of their mission to improve the lives of farmworkers, Huerta questioned the value of her assistance to the cause. Clearly, she underestimated her impact and the vital importance of her presence for Chávez and the farmworkers movement. The years 1962 to 1964 tested her resolve. She proved to be a steadfast defender of the social, political, and economic rights of agricultural laborers. In addition to abandoning her personal life, Huerta also sacrificed the comfort and ease of her family. Although several opportunities for better-paying positions came her way, she rejected them all in favor of devoting her energies to the establishment of the FWA. She had demonstrated to Chávez that she could be counted on, and he benefited from her loyalty, firmness of purpose, counsel, and honesty. Their friendship and partnership forged during these early years would lead to the achievement of many historic victories for farmworkers. Their alliance and commitment made in the early 1960s would sustain them in numerous battles on behalf of farm laborers for more than thirty years.

A key to Huerta's commitment to the farmworkers' movement rested on her assessment of Chávez. Her estimation of Chávez evolved over the late 1950s and early 1960s before the union had made national headlines. Prior to their formal introduction, Huerta had repeatedly heard of his notable organizational skills from Fred Ross. When Chávez and Huerta finally met, she was disappointed. He did not match her image of a dynamic, high-powered, larger-than-life individual. Speaking to a reporter, she recalled, "I didn't get a chance to talk to him the first time I met him, and he didn't make much of an impression on me."[19] Over the years, her earlier estimation changed. What progressively impressed her was his dedication, hard work, leadership style, and philosophy.

Reflecting on her initial reaction, she later remarked, "You couldn't tell by looking at him what he could do; you had to see him in action to appreciate him."[20] In the brief period 1962 to 1964, she saw Chávez's complete dedication to the farmworker cause. His modesty and lack of ego appealed to her. She became convinced that the unionization of farmworkers, and not self-promotion, was the motivating force driving him. Huerta admired his work ethic and concentration. He threw himself fully into organizing, even depriving his family of his personal attention and time.

Huerta also came to believe that she had underestimated his aptitude for leadership. Originally perceiving him as low-key and ordinary,

[19]Matthiessen, *Sal Si Puedes,* 50.
[20]Ibid.

she increasingly appreciated his simple but compelling style, his fairness, and his steadiness. She also prized the esteem he bestowed on colleagues. He did not ask anything of anyone that he was not willing to undertake himself. In her view, he sought and was willing to listen to different points of view. Huerta experienced this quality in their relationship. He perceived her as a coequal, not as a follower. Although they often disagreed, she felt the freedom to state her opinions. She also believed that he accepted her limitations and shortcomings. She gradually determined that his unassuming manner was a strength rather than a weakness. His brand of leadership projected a model of commitment, cooperation, perseverance, and integrity.

Above all, Huerta respected Chávez's core values, beliefs, and philosophy. In the early years of their partnership, she shared his view of the dignity of the individual, regardless of one's station in life. She observed firsthand his deep outrage at the exploitation of farmworkers and their families. She witnessed his fervent conviction that farm laborers had the power to change their own lives. She discovered his ability to adopt the tactic of nonviolence from the civil rights protests and adapt it to the farmworkers movement. These principles and faith in the mission provided the guidance and direction to lead La Causa during the difficult trials of bitter strikes, long fasts, prolonged boycotts, legal hurdles, and political obstacles that would challenge the union in the years to come.

FRANK BARDACKE

César's Ghost: Decline and Fall of the UFW

1993

Frank Bardacke, a public school teacher in California and a former employee of a vegetable-packing plant, points to Chávez's flawed leadership as a major reason for the decline of the UFW in the 1980s and early 1990s. Bardacke asserts that Chávez made a major mistake in arbitrarily and dogmatically pulling farmworkers out of the fields to picket and boycott in towns and cities. By doing so, he says, Chávez undercut his

---

Frank Bardacke, "Cesar's Ghost: Decline and Fall of the U.F.W.," *Nation*, 26 July/2 Aug. 1993, 130–35.

major source of support among field laborers and divided his followers. Because Chávez refused to listen to alternative suggestions and sometimes forced his critics out of the UFW, he increasingly lost support in the decade before his death in 1993. Bardacke's essay illustrates the views of journalists, historians, and biographers who, though praising Chávez's hard work and commitment to his causes, point to major shortcomings in his leadership style.

Cesar, who was always good at symbols, saved his best for last: a simple pine box, fashioned by his brother's hands, carried unceremoniously through the Central Valley town he made famous. With some 35,000 people looking on.

Here was meaning enough, both for those who need it blunt and for those who like it subtle. No one—especially not the newspaper and TV reporters whose liberal sympathies had been one of his main assets—could fail to hear that pine box speak: Cesar Chavez's commitment to voluntary poverty extended even unto death. And perhaps a few among the crowd would get the deeper reference. Burial insurance had been Cesar's first organizing tool in building the National Farmworkers Association back in 1962. Many farmworkers, then and now, die so badly in debt that they can't afford to be buried. By joining up with Cesar and paying dues to the association, workers earned the right to take their final rest in a pine box, built by brother Richard.

The funeral march and picnic were near perfect. The friendly crowd was primarily Chicano, people who had driven a couple of hours up and over the Grapevine from Los Angeles to honor the man who was the authentic representative of their political coming of age in postwar America. Martin Luther King is the standard comparison, but Cesar Chavez was King and Jackie Robinson, too. Chicanos and Mexicans had played well in their own leagues—they built a lot of power in the railroad, mining and factory unions of the Southwest—but Cesar forced his way into the political big leagues, where Chicanos had always been excluded. And, like Robinson, he played on his own terms.

Not only Chicanos but all manner of farmworker supporters marched at the funeral: liberal politicians, celebrities, Catholic priests, grape and lettuce boycotters. This was fitting too, as Chavez had always insisted that his greatest contribution to the farmworker movement was the consumer boycott. The boycott, he argued, ended the debilitating isolation of farmworkers that had doomed their earlier organizing. And so it was right that the boycotters marched at Cesar's funeral, and it was their buttons (the word "grapes" or "uvas"* with a ghostbuster line through it) that everyone wore.

What the march lacked was farmworkers, at least in mass numbers. Several buses had come down from the Salinas Valley, and farmworkers from the immediate area were well represented, but as a group, farmworkers added little weight to the funeral. I saw no banners from U.F.W. locals, nor did I see a single button or sign proclaiming the idea of farmworker power. And this, too, was symbolically perfect, for at the time of Cesar Chavez's death, the U.F.W. was not primarily a farmworker organization. It was a fundraising operation, run out of a deserted tuberculosis sanitarium in the Tehachapi Mountains, far from the fields of famous Delano, staffed by members of Cesar's extended family and using as its political capital Cesar's legend and the warm memories of millions of aging boycotters.

It was my second funeral march for Cesar Chavez. The first had been two days earlier, back home in Watsonville, in the Pajaro Valley, four and a half hours by car from Delano. Throughout the 1970s, Watsonville, together with nearby Salinas, had been a center of U.F.W. strength. Back then, most of the major growers (the two valleys specialize in vegetable row crops) were signed up with either the U.F.W. or the Teamsters, and pushed by the militancy of several hundred Chavistas, the two unions had won increasingly better contracts. In the 1980s the entry-level hourly wage moved up over $7, and working conditions on U.F.W. crews significantly improved. But by the end of the decade that had all come apart. In Watsonville, the U.F.W. now has only a couple of apple contracts, covering no more than a few hundred workers. In Salinas, the Teamsters still have a contract with the giant Bud Antle/Dole, but for most workers, unions have been replaced by farm labor contractors, and average hourly wages have fallen to around $5.

So I was surprised by the farmworker presence at that first funeral march. Fewer than 200 people had shown up, but a good number of them were field workers. I ran into my old friend Roberto Fernandez,[1] the man who taught me how to pack celery in the mid-seventies and who helped me make it on a piece-rate celery crew, where on good days we made over $15 an hour. Roberto came to California first as a

*uvas: Spanish word for grapes
[1] A pseudonym.

bracero in the early 1960s and later as an illegal. We worked side by side for three years, and I have a lot of memories of Roberto, but my fondest is when we were on a picket line together, trying to prevent a helicopter from spraying a struck field. We were with a group of other strikers, half-jokingly using slings to throw rocks at the helicopter as it flew past. Suddenly, Roberto ran into the field, directly at the oncoming helicopter, a baseball-size rock twirling in the sling above his head, screaming a warrior's roar. The rest of us were astounded; God knows what the pilot thought as he yanked the helicopter straight up and away from the kamikaze attack.

Roberto, his 6-year-old daughter and I walked a short while on the march together, and when the other folks went into Asunción Church to pray, the three of us walked back into town. I had seen Roberto off and on since I left our celery crew after the 1979 strike, but we had avoided discussing farmworker politics. Roberto is a committed Chavista and always could be counted on to give the official U.F.W. line. He was currently working on one of the few union contracts in town—not with the U.F.W. but with a rival independent union, as the U.F.W. no longer has any celery workers under contract. I asked him what went wrong in the fields.

"The Republicans replaced the Democrats and ruined the law, and we no longer had any support in Sacramento."

"That's it? All the power we had, gone just because Deukmejian replaced Brown?"

"The people were too ignorant."

"What do you mean?"

"We got swamped by people coming from small ranchos in Mexico who didn't know anything about unions. When the companies were letting our contracts expire and bringing in the labor contractors, we would go out to the people in the fields and try to explain to them about the union. But they didn't get it. They just wanted to work."

"I don't believe that. We had people from ranchos in Mexico on our U.F.W. crews. They were strong unionists; unions are not such a hard thing to understand."

"Well, Frank, you aren't ever going to believe that the workers were at fault, but I was there and I talked to them, and you weren't."

I never could beat Roberto in an argument, and although I like to think I would have had a better chance in English, probably not. Two days later I drove to Delano with another old friend, Cruz Gomez. Cruz's father was a farmworker—a year-round employee on a good-size farm outside Santa Barbara. The family was relatively well off compared with the braceros and the other seasonals who worked on the ranch. Nevertheless, her father worked thirty-seven years without a paid vacation, his body slowly breaking down as he passed middle age. As we were driving, I asked Cruz about Chavez.

"For me, Chavez was it, that's all, just it. He was the main man. I remember when I met him. It was 1967 or '68, I was a college student at the University of California at Santa Barbara. I was divorced and had two small children, a kind of mother figure in the MEChA [Movimiento Estudiantil Chicano de Aztlan] student organization. We went up to Delano as a group, and sat around and talked with him. It was very informal, but he was all there. He gave us his full attention."

When Cruz returned to U.C.S.B. she, as they say, had been organized. She soon switched majors from biology to sociology, where a few influential teachers taught her that it was her obligation to "give back to the community." In 1971 she found herself working in a local community organization. She has been doing the same kind of work ever since, moving to Watsonville in 1978, spending her days listening to the problems of migrant farmworkers.

Unlike so many others with similar backgrounds, Cruz had never gone to work in Delano or even spent much time working in a boycott organization. From her contact with farmworkers she was well aware that the U.F.W. had become pretty much a nonfactor in the Pajaro and Salinas valleys, but she had no idea why. She asked me what had happened.

Roberto and the U.F.W. are not far wrong. The virtual destruction of a unionized work force in the fields of California in the 1980s was due finally to the overwhelming social, financial and political power of the biggest business in our Golden State. The weight of the internal errors of the U.F.W. is secondary to the longstanding anti-union policies of the people who own and operate the most powerful agro-export industry in the world.

Nevertheless, in the late seventies, at the height of the U.F.W.'s strength among farmworkers, some in California agribusiness had come to the conclusion that Chavez's victory was inevitable and that they would have to learn to live with the U.F.W. Why wasn't the union—with perhaps 50,000 workers under contract and hundreds of militant activists among them—able to seize this historic opportunity?

The short answer is that within the U.F.W. the boycott tail came to wag the farmworker dog. While it was not wrong of Chavez to seek as much support as possible, this support work, primarily the boycott, became the essential activity of the union. Ultimately, it interfered with organizing in the fields.

It was an easy mistake to fall into, especially as the failure of the first grape strikes was followed so stunningly by the success of the first grape boycott. The very best farmworker activists, the strongest Chavistas, were removed from the fields and direct contact with farmworkers, so that they could be sent to work in the boycott offices of major cities. From the point of view of building the boycott, it was a genius decision. But from the point of view of spreading the union among farmworkers themselves, it was a disaster.

The manipulative use of farmworkers gave the union boycott its texture and feel. In the mid-1970s a story circulated in Salinas about a union meeting in the Imperial Valley called to recruit workers to go to a press conference in Los Angeles to support one of the boycotts. For the workers it meant a ten-hour round-trip drive on one of their days off, but many of them were willing to do it. These particular farmworkers were mostly young piece-rate lettuce cutters who earned relatively high wages, and who, like a lot of working-class people able to afford it, put their money into clothes and cars which they sported on their days off. They were proud people, volunteering to spend a weekend in Los Angeles organizing support for their movement. As the meeting closed, Marshall Ganz—one of the union's top officials at the time—had a final request. At the press conference everybody should wear their *work* clothes.

The union officials didn't want farmworkers to appear as regular working people appealing for solidarity. They had to be poor and suffering, hats in hand, asking for charity. It may have made a good press conference, but the people who told the story were angered and shamed.

What the U.F.W. called publicity strikes hurt quite a bit too. Typically, the union would enter a small spontaneous walkout (a tactic California farmworkers have been using for more than a hundred years to drive up wages at harvest time), escalate local demands as a way of publicizing the overall plight of farmworkers and then leave. This played well enough in New York and Chicago, but made it more difficult for farmworkers to win these local battles.

The union's strategy after passage of California's Agricultural [Labor] Relations Act in 1975 was similar. The union would aim to win as many certification elections as possible, thereby demonstrating to Governor Jerry Brown, allies in the California legislature, boycott supporters around the world and even agribusiness that it had the allegiance of a large majority of California farmworkers. The U.F.W.

hoped that this would result in some sort of statewide master agreement, imposed from above, that would cover farmworkers in most of the larger agribusiness companies.

As with the publicity strikes, the U.F.W. came onto a ranch with its high-powered organizing techniques, explained how important it was for people to vote for the union, usually won the elections and then left. Less than a third of the elections resulted in union contracts, however; too many workers felt used and deserted; and opposition to the U.F.W. grew in the fields.

Just how out of touch the U.F.W. was with farmworker sentiment is perhaps best illustrated by its approach to the question of undocumented workers. Most all California farmworkers have people in their families who have trouble with their legal status, so any union trying to organize them cannot risk taking the side of the I.N.S. [Immigration and Naturalization Service], the hated *migra*. Yet the U.F.W. sometimes supported the use of the *migra* against scabs, sacrificing long-term respect for a possible short-term gain.

It was the lack of strength among farmworkers that made the 1983 change in the Governor's office and the weakening of boycott support so devastating. Some of the biggest ranches reorganized their operations and replaced union contracts with labor contractors. Others let their U.F.W. contracts expire and refused to renegotiate them. In both cases, the union was powerless to stop them; the years of neglecting farmworker organizing finally took their toll.

A natural question arises: How could a farmworker organization staffed by so many intelligent people of good will, and led by one of the heroes of our time, make so many mistakes? The answer is just as direct. Structurally, the U.F.W. is one of the least democratic unions in the country. Officials in the local field offices are not elected by the workers under contract in those areas, as they are in most other unions. They are appointed by the U.F.W. executive board and were under the direct control of Cesar.

This meant that local farmworker leadership had no way of advancing within the union, other than by being personally loyal to Cesar or other high-level officials. Complaints about the union and its practices, although freely discussed among workers on the job, could not influence union policy.

This criticism does not fall from some idealized heaven of union democracy. Many staff members, who either resigned or were purged from the union, have complained privately about Chavez's authoritarian style and the lack of democracy within the U.F.W. They have rarely gone public, however, because they believed that any criticism of the U.F.W. would only help the growers, and because they were intimidated into silence by Chavez himself or by others on the U.F.W. staff. Even now people are reluctant to speak for fear of reprisals.

Philip Vera Cruz, onetime vice president of the union, who worked in the grapes for twenty years before Chavez came along, is the only staff member who put his criticism into print. Vera Cruz, who could not be guilt-tripped into silence, describes in an oral history, taken by Craig Scharlin and Lilia Villanueva, a U.F.W. staff where "power was held by Cesar alone." His conclusion is straightforward:

> One thing the union would never allow was for people to criticize Cesar. If a union leader is built up as a symbol and he talks like he was God, then there is no way you can have true democracy in the union because the members are just generally deprived of their right to reason for themselves.

The most critical U.F.W. purge was not against the union staff but against its own farmworker members—people who dared to give the union some alternative, middle-level leadership. The trouble began when the 1979 contracts provided for full-time union grievers, elected by the workers, to handle specific complaints from the work crews. Some of the people elected in Salinas, the first workers in the hierarchy to have any real power independent of Chavez, regularly criticized several internal union policies.

At the union's 1981 convention in Fresno these men and women supported three independent candidates, not previously approved by Chavez, for election to the U.F.W.'s executive board. Afterward, they were fired from their jobs back in Salinas. Although they eventually won a nearly five-year court battle against Chavez and the union, the damage was done. No secondary leadership emerging from the ranks would be tolerated in the U.F.W.

I talked to one of the men, Aristeo Zambrano, a few weeks after the funeral. Aristeo was one of eleven children born to a farmworker family in Chavinda, Michoacán. His father worked as a bracero between 1945 and 1960, and after getting his papers fixed, he brought his son, then 14, to Hayward, California, in 1969. Aristeo moved to Salinas in 1974 and got a job cutting broccoli at a U.F.W.-organized company—Associated Produce. He was elected to the ranch committee in 1976; for the next six years he was an active unionist, re-elected to the committee every year and then to the position of paid representative, until he was fired by Chavez.

I asked him the same question I had asked Roberto Fernandez. What went wrong? How did the union fall so far so fast? His answer took several hours. Here are a few minutes of it.

"The problem developed way before we were fired in 1982. In the mid-seventies, when I became an activist, Chavez was making every decision in the union. If a car in Salinas needed a new tire, we had to check with Cesar in La Paz. He controlled every detail of union business. And nobody was allowed to say Chavez made a mistake, even when he had. And when you talked to him you had to humble yourself, as if he were a King or the Pope. . . .

"I remember in particular a closed meeting during the strike, just before the Salinas convention in 1979. He called together about twenty of us—the elected picket captains and strike coordinators—and told us that he was going to call off the strike and send us on the boycott. We refused, and we told him so. We thought the strike should be extended, not called off. And we damn sure were not going on any boycott.

"Well, he couldn't call off the strike without our support, and we did continue to fight and we won. Which made us stronger. That meeting, and its aftermath, was a political challenge to Cesar. It meant that the situation in the union had changed. He was going to have to deal with us—with the direct representatives of the workers—and, in some way or other, share power with us.

"And that was what he couldn't do. He was incapable of sharing power. So after the 1982 convention—the first U.F.W. convention that was not simply a staged show, the first convention where true disagreements came to the floor—he fired us. First he tried to organize recall elections, so that farmworkers would replace us. But he couldn't do it. We had too much support in the field.

"We went back to the fields, and tried to continue organizing, but it impossible. The damage had been done. People were scared or gave up on the union. They could see that the union did not belong to the workers, that it was Chavez's own personal business, and that he would run his business as he pleased. Farmworkers were good for boycotting, or walking the picket lines, or paying union dues, but not for leading our union. . . .

"Chavez built the union and then he destroyed it. The U.F.W. self-destructed. When the Republicans came back in the 1980s and the growers moved against the union, there wasn't any farmworker movement left."

*   *   *

What happens next? There was a feeling of optimism at the funeral. So many people together again, united by their respect for Chavez, pledging themselves to renewed effort. In her own fashion, Dolores Huerta, one of the founders of the union, expressed the hope of the crowd in her eulogy. "Cesar," she said, "died in peace, in good health, with a serene look on his face. It was as if he had chosen to die at this time . . . at this Easter time. . . . He died so that we would wake up. He died so that the union might live."

In the several weeks since the funeral, I have pondered Dolores's image of Chavez as the U.F.W.'s Christ, dying so that we might live. In one way, it is perfect. All the talk of [Saul] Alinsky and community organizing aside, Cesar Chavez was essentially a lay Catholic leader. His deepest origins were not in Alinsky's radical Community Service Organization but in the *cursillos de Cristiandad* movement, the intense encounters of Catholic lay people, first developed by the clergy in Franco's Spain and transplanted to the New World in the 1950s. The song they brought with them was "De Colores," and their ideology was a combination of anticommunism and personal commitment of ordinary lay people to the Gospel's version of social justice. Chavez, throughout his public life, remained true to that commitment. What many of the liberals and radicals on the staff of the union could never understand was that all the fasts, the long marches, the insistence on personal sacrifice and the flirting with sainthood were not only publicity gimmicks, they were the essential Chavez.

Chavez died so that the union might live? What Dolores seems to have meant was that people, inspired by Chavez's life, would now rejoin the cause and rebuild the union. That might happen, but rebuilding the union *among farmworkers* will require a complete break with the recent past by the people who now control the U.F.W.

The U.F.W. is no longer the only group trying to organize in the fields of California. Teamster Local 890 in Salinas, with more than 7,000 field workers under contract, recently has been taken over by reformers with long experience in the Chicano and Mexican cannery worker movement. They would like to begin a new organizing drive in the Salinas Valley. In Stockton, Luis Magaña and the Organización Laboral Agrícola de California have established close contacts with the newest migrant stream in California agriculture, the Mixtec and Zapotec Indians from Oaxaca. In many areas small community groups have gone beyond simply providing services to farmworkers and have helped them organize to fight for better housing, better schooling for their kids, and against violations of labor laws by farmworker contractors.

Up until now, these small beginnings have had an uneasy relation-ship with the U.F.W. Viewing them as competitive organizations, Chavez often tried to block their activities, even when the U.F.W. was not organizing in the same areas. Now that Chavez is gone, could the U.F.W. learn to cooperate with these other groups? Could people who were originally inspired by the heroic example of Chavez's life, and who now no longer have Cesar around to interfere with their work, make a hundred flowers bloom in the California fields?

*Sí se puede.**

*Sí se puede: Yes, it can happen.

PETER MATTHIESSEN

César Chávez

1993

Peter Matthiessen, a well-known journalist and the author of a book on Chávez and the farmworkers, attempts to sum up the meaning of Chávez's life. Matthiessen captures Chávez's significance in the marriage of two complementary urges—the "gentle mystic" linked to the "relentless labor leader." Chávez could inspire his followers with his fasts and his Catholic spirituality, but he could also organize and lead his followers in strikes, boycotts, and a massive labor movement. Matthiessen sides with those who think of Chávez as one of the most important Americans of the twentieth century.

Cesar Chavez was on union business when his life ended quietly in his sleep, at 10:30 or 11 P.M. on April 22nd, in the small border town of San Luis, Arizona, thirty-five miles and sixty-six years distant from the childhood farm in the Gila River Valley which his parents lost at the end of the Depression. On April 29th, in ninety-degree heat, an esti-mated thirty-five thousand people, in a line three miles long, formed a funeral procession from Memorial Park in Delano, California, to the burial Mass, at the United Farm Workers field office north of town.

With the former scourge of California safely in his coffin, state flags were lowered to half-mast by order of the governor, and messages

Peter Matthiessen, "Cesar Chavez," *New Yorker,* 17 May 1993, 82.

poured forth from the heads of church and state, including the Pope and the President of the United States. This last of the U.F.W. marches was greater, even, than the 1975 march against the Gallo winery, which helped destroy the growers' cynical alliance with the Teamsters. "We have lost perhaps the greatest Californian of the twentieth century," the president of the California State Senate said, in public demotion of Cesar Chavez's sworn enemies Nixon and Reagan.

For most of his life, Cesar Estrada Chavez chose to live penniless and without property, devoting everything he had, including his frail health, to the U.F.W., the first effective farmworkers' union ever created in the United States. "Without a union, the people are always cheated, and they are so innocent," Chavez told me when we first met, in July, 1968, in Delano, where he lived with his wife, Helen, and a growing family. Chavez, five feet six, and a sufferer from recurrent back pain, seemed an unlikely David to go up against the four-billion-dollar Goliath of California agribusiness. Not until January, 1968, after many hard years of door-to-door organizing of uneducated and intimidated migrant workers, had his new independent union felt strong enough to attempt a nationwide boycott of table grapes, publicized by the first of many prolonged religious fasts. On July 29, 1970, the main Delano growers all but ended the boycott by signing union contracts with the U.F.W.

This historic victory was no sooner won when the U.F.W. was challenged by the Teamsters Union, which rushed in to sign up lettuce workers in the Salinas Valley. Chavez was angered by the perfidy of the growers, who were bent on conspiring with the Teamsters to steal from behind the U.F.W.'s back what it had won in a fair, hard fight. He also resented the hostility of almost all municipal and state officials, from the ubiquitous police to Governor Reagan, which exposed his farmworkers to an unrestrained climate of violence and took the lives of five U.F.W. members in the course of strikes and organizing campaigns. For Chavez, that hostility led to a resurfacing of emotional injuries he had suffered as a child, all the way back to the bank foreclosure on the small family farm and the brutal racism in such signs as "No Dogs or Mexicans Allowed." "Getting rejected hurts very deep," he told me once, recalling a time in Indio, California, during his migrant days when he followed his father into a decrepit diner to buy morning coffee, only to be contemptuously ordered out. To this day, he said, he could remember the expression on his father's face, and though it has been twenty years or more since Cesar told me that story, I can still recall his expression when he told it—that seraphic

Indian face with the dark, sad, soft eyes and delighted smile turned crude and ugly.

In recent years, beset by the unremitting prejudice of California's Republican administrations, which were elected with the strong support of agribusiness, the embittered Chavez embarked upon a table-grape and lettuce boycott against nonunion growers, protesting the use of dangerous pesticides, which threaten the health not only of farmworkers but of the public. The new boycott never took hold. What was lacking seemed to be the fervor of those exhilarating marches under union flags, the fasts, the singing, and the chanting—*"Viva la huelga!"*—that put the fear of God in the rich farm owners of California. These brilliant tactics remained tied in the public perception to La Causa, a labor and civil-rights movement with religious overtones which rose to prominence in the feverish tumult of the sixties; as a mature A.F.L.-C.I.O. union, the U.F.W. lost much of its symbolic power. Membership has now declined to about one-fifth of its peak of a hundred thousand.

With the funeral march over, the highway empty, and all the banners put away, Cesar Chavez's friends and perhaps his foes are wondering what will become of the U.F.W. A well-trained new leadership (his son-in-law has been named to succeed him, and four of his eight children work for the union) may bring fresh energy and insight. But what the union will miss is Chavez's spiritual fire. A man so unswayed by money, a man who (despite many death threats) refused to let his bodyguards go armed, and who offered his entire life to the service of others, was not to be judged by the same standards of some self-serving labor leader or politician. Self-sacrifice lay at the very heart of the devotion he inspired, and gave dignity and hope not only to the farmworkers but to every one of the Chicano people, who saw for themselves what one brave man, indifferent to his own health and welfare, could accomplish.

Anger was a part of Chavez, but so was a transparent love of humankind. The gentle mystic that his disciples wished to see inhabited the same small body as the relentless labor leader who concerned himself with the most minute operation of his union. Astonishingly— this seems to me his genius—the two Cesars were so complementary that without either, La Causa could not have survived.

During the vigil at the open casket on the day before the funeral, an old man lifted a child up to show him the small, gray-haired man who lay inside. "I'm going to tell you about this man someday," he said.

PART FIVE

Seeing a Life Whole

A César Chávez Chronology: 1927–1993

1927   March 31: César Estrada Chávez is born to Librado and Juana Chávez in Yuma, Arizona.

1937   Chávez family becomes field workers in California.

1944–46   Chávez serves in the U.S. Navy.

1948   Chávez marries Helen Fabela, a native of Delano, California, in October. They eventually have eight children.

Late 1940s   César and Helen Chávez move to San Jose, California.

Early 1950s   Chávez becomes an organizer for the Community Service Organization (CSO).

1957   Chávez meets Dolores Huerta, who will become his most trusted lieutenant in labor organizing.

1958   Chávez is named a national director of the CSO.

1962   Chávez resigns from the CSO, moves to Delano, and begins to organize a farmworkers union. He founds the Farm Workers Association (FWA), which is also called the National Farm Workers Association (NFWA).

1964   The NWA officially becomes the NFWA.

1965   The famed Delano strike begins; it will continue for five years.

1966   Chávez leads an Easter march to Sacramento, California. The NFWA joins another group of field workers to become the United Farm Workers Organizing Committee (UFWOC), but the new group is popularly called the United Farm Workers (UFW).

1968   Chávez undertakes a twenty-five-day fast. On the day he breaks the fast, he meets with Robert Kennedy.

1970   Delano strike ends; contracts are signed with several major growers.

1972   UFWOC officially becomes the United Farm Workers (UFW).

1975   California legislature enacts collective bargaining for farmworkers in the state.

1980s   Chávez faces mounting opposition from conservative political leaders nationally and in California.

1984   Chávez announces a grape and lettuce boycott; he uses direct-mail methods.

1985   Poll in California indicates that 53 percent of the people support Chávez; only 21 percent oppose him.

Late 1980s   Chávez continues his efforts for higher wages and increased benefits for workers and against the excessive use of pesticides in the fields.

1991   UFW loses a $2 million court case for damages resulting from a 1979 strike in California.

1993   April 23: Chávez dies in his sleep in Arizona.

Making Connections

Discussion questions appearing earlier in this volume will help readers to think analytically about those selections. But like a conversation, the selections also speak to one another. The questions that follow will help readers to see Chávez's career as a whole, complex, multifaceted life.

1. Which of César Chávez's personal characteristics appealed most to his farmworkers? To others?
2. What were the major reasons for Chávez's success as a leader?
3. Some of Chávez's supporters viewed him as a hero—as a man above and beyond other people. How do you react to this view?
4. Chávez was clearly a religious man. What religious ideas seemed to influence him most? How did he exhibit his own spirituality?
5. Ethnically, Chávez was a Mexican American and a Chicano. Do you think his ethnic identity was more or less influential in shaping his life than his working-class and religious backgrounds?

6. Historians have written often about the concept of a "citizen" or "citizenship." How would you define these terms, and how might they apply to Chávez?
7. What accomplishment in Chávez's career would you point to as his most outstanding achievement?

Research Opportunities

Using the materials in this book and information gathered from additional research in sources listed in part six, students should be able to prepare brief, analytical papers on Chávez's life. These essays might focus on any of the following questions.

1. Mexican women played signal roles in Chávez's career. Why do you think this was so?
2. Can you compare Chávez's leadership style to that of Martin Luther King Jr.? How were they similar and different?
3. If you were to write an essay titled "The Legacies of César Chávez," which legacies would you emphasize?
4. Historians and others writing about Chávez often point to his successes in the 1960s and 1970s and his disappointments thereafter. How would you account for the ups and downs of his career?
5. Some commentators speak of Chávez as a major figure in America during the second half of the twentieth century. Do you see him as a notable figure in American history? Why or why not?

PART SIX

Sources for a Life:
Selected Bibliography

Writings on César Chávez, farmworkers, and the Chicano Movement have notably proliferated during the past three decades. Although the first studies tended to focus on Chávez the man and his work as a labor organizer, more recent books and essays treat broader, contextual subjects. The following listing, intended for students, instructors, and scholars interested in pursuing any of these topics, is divided into three parts: sources on Chávez, his followers, and his advisers; books and essays on the larger Chicano Movement; and books and dissertations dealing with Chávez's ideas, as well as those of other Mexican Americans and Chicanos, all part of a burgeoning Chicano citizenry.

César Chávez: The Man and His Circle

Three books are beginning points for an understanding of Chávez the man, his participation in Chicano culture, and his ideas and activities. For an extensive, firsthand source on Chávez's early years, his initial efforts as an organizer, and his rapid rise to the leadership of the Mexican American farmworkers, start with Jacques E. Levy, *Cesar Chavez: Autobiography of La Causa* (New York: W. W. Norton, 1975). This lengthy volume contains numerous interviews with Chávez, his wife and friends, his fellow organizers, and his opponents. But the book must not be considered an exact, word-for-word account of these interviews, since Levy chose "what is left out as well as what is included"

124 SOURCES FOR A LIFE

(p. xvii). "Sometimes," Levy writes, "I blend his [Chávez's] remarks from several sources to bring out his views" (p. xvii). Even after these limitations are considered, this thorough volume remains an indispensable source on Chávez and the UFW through the mid-1970s.

The most valuable biography of Chávez is Richard Griswold del Castillo and Richard A. Garcia, *César Chávez: A Triumph of Spirit* (Norman: University of Oklahoma Press, 1995). This compact, clearly written life story is the best account of Chávez and his links to the Chicano Movement. The authors are particularly adept at delineating Chávez's personality, his spiritual and moral dimensions, and his place in Mexican American history from the 1950s to the 1990s.

A third valuable source is Susan Ferriss and Ricardo Sandoval, *The Fight in the Fields: Cesar Chavez and the Farmworkers Movement* (New York: Harcourt Brace, 1997). Prepared as a companion to the documentary film *The Fight in the Fields,* this smoothly written volume is based on sound research in pertinent primary and secondary sources. It also relies on numerous oral interviews and unpublished documents. This lively book will be helpful for scholars and students alike.

Several journalists and other writers, some with firsthand knowledge of the dramatic events they narrate, have written book-length accounts of Chávez and the famous Delano strike (1965–70). Freelance journalist Eugene Nelson, the son of a grape grower, converted to the farmworker cause and wrote an early sympathetic account of the strike in *Huelga: The First Hundred Days of the Great Delano Grape Strike* (Delano, Calif.: Farm Worker Press, 1966). Published one year later was John Gregory Dunne's *Delano: The Story of the California Grape Strike* (New York: Farrar, Straus and Giroux, 1967). This book, the most literary of these early works, is replete with firsthand observations and information gained from numerous interviews. It is insightful and delightfully written. Also rewarding as a work of literature is Peter Matthiessen, *Sal Si Puedes: Cesar Chavez and the New American Revolution* (1969; reprint, Berkeley: University of California Press, 2000). This volume was probably the most widely circulated of the initial books about Chávez. Descriptive, evocative, and filled with sharp character studies, it remains one of the most valuable studies of Chávez, with Matthiessen's skills as a novelist clearly empowering his narrative.

Chávez and his farmworkers are placed in historical context in Joan London and Henry Anderson, *So Shall Ye Reap: The Story of Cesar Chavez and the Farm Workers' Movement* (New York: Thomas Y.

Crowell, 1970). Anderson, a journalist, and London, the daughter of famed novelist Jack London, provide useful background on the earlier labor movements on which Chávez built his efforts. Similar journalistic accounts include Ronald B. Taylor, *Chavez and the Farm Workers* (Boston: Beacon Press, 1975), and Dick Meister and Anne Loftis, *A Long Time Coming: The Struggle to Unionize America's Farm Workers* (New York: Macmillan, 1977). Both are smoothly written, anecdotal, and readable. Taylor focuses more on Chávez, and Meister and Loftis place him and his farmworkers in a national context. Sam Kushner, *Long Road to Delano* (New York: International Publishers, 1975), views the events from a leftist perspective.

Some of Chávez's fellow organizers and others influential in the UFW have also furnished accounts of their work with him. The most important of these are books by Mark Day and Fred Ross. Day's *Forty Acres: Cesar Chavez and the Farm Workers* (New York: Praeger Publishers, 1971) tells the story from the point of view of a Catholic priest close to Chávez in the late 1960s. Day also edited *El Malcriado,* the UFW's newspaper and the primary source of information on Chávez and the UFW. Ross's *Conquering Goliath: César Chávez at the Beginning* (Keene, Calif.: El Taller Grafico, 1989), a reckoning by the organizer who may have been the most influential force on Chávez in the early years, is a collection of remembered conversations and events twenty to thirty years after they took place.

Over the years, several writers have also provided stories of Chávez and the farmworkers for younger readers. Among these are Consuelo Rodriguez, *Cesar Chavez,* Hispanics of Achievement (New York: Chelsea House Publishers, 1991), and David R. Collins, *Farmworker's Friend: The Story of Cesar Chavez* (Minneapolis: Carolrhoda Books, 1966).

Other scholarly books, though not meant as biographies, provide helpful information on Chávez and his circle of friends and coworkers. John C. Hammerback and Richard J. Jensen, *The Rhetorical Career of César Chávez* (College Station: Texas A & M University Press, 1998), intended as a study of Chávez's published and manuscript speeches, also contains much little-known and infrequently cited information on Chávez. This volume includes a particularly notable bibliography of writings by and about Chávez. J. Craig Jenkins, *The Politics of Insurgency: The Farm Worker Movement in the 1960s* (New York: Columbia University Press, 1985), is a pioneering scholarly monograph. It is solidly researched and based on a thorough use of important published and manuscript sources, with about half its pages devoted to a probing discussion of Chávez and the UFW.

César Chávez and the Chicano Movement

A large number of books treat the larger contexts of Chávez's career. Some provide useful background on Mexican American experiences before the 1960s, others furnish comparisons between Chávez and other Chicano leaders, and still others supply helpful studies of the larger Chicano Movement in the second half of the twentieth century.

Readers interested in Mexican American experiences prior to the 1960s should begin with the superb writings of journalist/lawyer/historian Carey McWilliams. His classic work, *North from Mexico: The Spanish-Speaking People of the United States* (Philadelphia: J. B. Lippincott, 1948), remains a valuable source more than a half century after its publication. Also helpful is McWilliams's *Factories in the Field: The Story of Migratory Farm Labor in California* (Boston: Little, Brown, 1939). For an account by an author even closer to farmworker experiences, see Ernesto Galarza, *Merchants of Labor: The Mexican Bracero Story* (Charlotte, Calif.: McNally and Loftin, 1964). Two recent scholarly monographs cover much of the same ground, but from different perspectives. See Camille Guerin-Gonzales, *Mexican Workers and American Dreams: Immigration, Repatriation, and California Farm Labor, 1900–1939* (New Brunswick, N.J.: Rutgers University Press, 1994), and George J. Sánchez, *Becoming Mexican American: Ethnicity, Culture and Identity in Chicano Los Angeles, 1900–1945* (New York: Oxford University Press, 1993). Cletus E. Daniel, *Bitter Harvest: A History of California Farm Workers, 1870–1941* (Ithaca, N.Y.: Cornell University Press, 1981), provides valuable background for the UFW's story.

Several other authors deal with well-known Chicano leaders who were contemporaries of Chávez. A useful study of New Mexico's fiery Reies López Tijerina is Richard Gardner, *¡Grito! Reies Tijerina and the New Mexico Land Grant War of 1967* (Indianapolis: Bobbs-Merrill, 1970). On José Angel Gutiérrez and his work with the political organization La Raza Unida, see John Staples Shockley, *Chicano Revolt in a Texas Town* (Notre Dame, Ind.: University of Notre Dame Press, 1974), and on Denver activist Rodolfo "Corky" Gonzales, see Christine Marín, *A Spokesman of the Mexican American Movement: Rodolfo "Corky" Gonzales and the Fight for Chicano Liberation, 1966–1972* (San Francisco: R and E Research Associates, 1977).

We still lack a full-length study of Chicana leaders in the Movement. Until that book is published, researchers should use pertinent discussions in Alfredo Mirandé and Evangelica Enríquez, *La Chicana: The Mexican-American Woman* (Chicago: University of Chicago Press, 1979), and the appropriate sections of Vicki Ruiz's superb recent overview, *From Out of the Shadows: Mexican Women in Twentieth-Century America* (New York: Oxford University Press, 1998). The most extensive work on women's involvement in the UFW is Margaret Eleanor Rose, "Women in the United Farm Workers: A Study of Chicana and Mexicana Participation in a Labor Union, 1950 to 1980" (Ph.D. diss., University of California, Los Angeles, 1988). Part of Rose's findings are published in her useful essay "Traditional and Nontraditional Patterns of Female Activism in the United Farm Workers of America, 1962 to 1980," *Frontiers* 11 (No. 1, 1990): 26–32.

Numerous books are available on the Chicano Movement. On this large subject, begin with the books of the senior Chicano historian, Juan Gómez-Quiñones. Among his many strong works, see especially *Chicano Politics: Reality and Promise, 1940–1990* (Albuquerque: University of New Mexico Press, 1990), and *Mexican American Labor, 1790–1990* (Albuquerque: University of New Mexico Press, 1994). Nearly all the major overviews of Chicano history also contain sections on the Chicano Movement. Consult, for example, the pertinent discussions in the outspoken book by Rodolfo Acuña, *Occupied America: A History of Chicanos,* 4th ed. (New York: Longman, 2000). Less activist in tone and orientation but of equal help are Matt S. Meier and Feliciano Ribera, *Mexican Americans/American Mexicans: From Conquistadors to Chicanos,* rev ed. (New York: Hill and Wang, 1993), and Richard Griswold del Castillo and Arnoldo de León, *North to Aztlán: A History of Mexican Americans in the United States* (New York: Twayne Publishers, 1997). The most recent overview is Oscar Martínez, *Mexican-Origin People in the United States: A Topical History* (Tucson: University of Arizona Press, 2001). Also useful is Carlos Muñoz, *Youth, Identity, Power: The Chicano Generation* (New York: Verso, 1989).

César Chávez: Chicano Citizen

Chávez did not publish widely about his ideas and personal values. Yet there are extensive discussions of his labor activities, family and religious values, and political stances in the previously mentioned books by Jacques Levy, Richard Griswold del Castillo and Richard A. Garcia, and Susan Ferriss and Ricardo Sandoval. Hammerback and Jensen,

The Rhetorical Career of César Chávez, also contains a thorough listing of Chávez's writings, speeches, and interviews, as well as major books and essays written about him. In fact, nearly all the books cited in the first section of this bibliography contain illuminating treatments of Chávez's ideological positions.

Three doctoral dissertations deal with the religious ideas/spirituality of Chávez. See Luis D. León, "Religious Movement in the United States–Mexican Borderlands: Toward a Theory of Chicana/o Religious Poetics" (Ph.D. diss., University of California, Santa Barbara, 1997); Alan J. Watt, "The Religious Dimensions in the Farm Worker Movement" (Ph.D. diss., Vanderbilt University, 1999); and Frederick John Dalton, "The Moral Vision of César E. Chávez: An Examination of His Public Life from an Ethical Perspective" (Ph.D. diss., Graduate Theological Union, 1998).

Several other books provide revealing comparisons of Chávez and the larger contexts of Chicano social, economic, and political themes. See, for example, the smoothly written study by David G. Gutiérrez, *Walls and Mirrors: Mexican Americans, Mexican Immigrants, and the Politics of Ethnicity* (Berkeley: University of California Press, 1995), which clarifies important differences between Mexican Americans and immigrants from Mexico. Also of note is David R. Maciel and Isidro D. Ortiz, eds., *Chicanas/Chicanos at the Crossroads: Social, Economic, and Political Change* (Tucson: University of Arizona Press, 1996). For a discussion of an earlier period of Chicano thought and action, one should examine Mario T. García, *Mexican Americans: Leadership, Ideology, and Identity* (New Haven, Conn.: Yale University Press, 1989).

Finally, for those students looking for additional listings of books and essays on Chávez, the farmworkers, and the Chicano Movement, several bibliographies are available. Dated but still useful is Beverly Fodell, *Cesar Chavez and the United Farm Workers: A Selective Bibliography* (Detroit: Wayne State University Press, 1974). Also helpful are Matt S. Meier, *Bibliography of Mexican American History* (Westport, Conn.: Greenwood Press, 1984); Albert Camarillo, *Latinos in the United States: A Historical Bibliography* (Santa Barbara, Calif.: ABC-Clio, 1986); and Jacqueline J. Etulain, comp., *Mexican Americans in the Twentieth-Century American West: A Bibliography* (Albuquerque: Center for the American West, University of New Mexico, 1990).

Acknowledgments (continued from p. iv)

Frank Bardacke, *Cesar's Ghost: Decline and Fall of the UFW,* is reprinted with permission from the July 26, 1993, issue of *The Nation.*

César Chávez, "The Mexican-American and the Church," from Octavio Ignacio Romano-V, ed., *Voices: Readings from El Grito: A Journal of Contemporary Mexican American Thought, 1967–1973.* Reprinted by permission of Quinto Sol Publications.

César Chávez, "The Organizer's Tale," from Renato Rosaldo, Robert A. Calvert, and Gustav L. Seligmann, eds., *Chicano: The Evolution of a People.* Reprinted by permission of the Winston Press, Minneapolis.

Richard Griswold del Castillo, "The Birth of La Causa," from Richard Griswold del Castillo and Richard A. Garcia, *César Chávez: A Triumph of the Spirit.* Copyright © 1995 by the University of Oklahoma Press, Norman. Reprinted by permission.

Jacques Levy, *Cesar Chavez: Autobiography of La Causa,* pp. 112–13, 128, 147–48, 162–63, 246, 277–78, 293, 429–30, 489–90, 533–34. Reprinted with the permission of the author, Jacques E. Levy.

Peter Matthiessen, *César Chávez,* is reprinted with permission of the author.

Studs Turkel, "Cesar Chavez," in *Hard Times: An Oral History of the Great Depression.* Courtesy of Random House, Inc.

Index